CAPTAIN JACK'S COMPLETE NAVIGATION

JACK I. DAVIS

Editor: John P. Kaufman

BRISTOL FASHION PUBLICATIONS
Rockledge, Florida

Captain Jack's Complete Navigation, By Jack I. Davis

Published by Bristol Fashion Publications

Copyright © 1999 by Jack I. Davis. All rights reserved.

No part of this book may be reproduced or used in any form or by any means-graphic, electronic, mechanical, including photocopying, recording, taping or information storage and retrieval systems-without written permission of the publisher.

BRISTOL FASHION PUBLICATIONS AND THE AUTHOR HAVE MADE EVERY EFFORT TO INSURE THE ACCURACY OF THE INFORMATION PROVIDED IN THIS BOOK BUT ASSUMES NO LIABILITY WHATSOEVER FOR SAID INFORMATION OR THE CONSEQUENCES OF USING THE INFORMATION PROVIDED IN THIS BOOK.

ISBN: 1-892216-25-6
LCCN: 99-75392

Contribution acknowledgments

Cover art and inside illustrations by Joe Kolb, unless otherwise indicated.
Cover design by John P. Kaufman.

Captain Jack's Complete Navigation, By Jack I. Davis

Captain Jack's Complete Navigation, By Jack I. Davis

Captain Jack's Complete Navigation, By Jack I. Davis

TABLE OF CONTENTS

PART ONE
BASIC NAVIGATION

Introduction   Page 13

Chapter 1
Distance, Speed and Time   Page 19
Distance, Speed and Time Answers   Page 28

Chapter 2
Learn to Sail   Page 31

Chapter 3
Compass   Page 33
Compass Answers   Page 47

Chapter 4
To Be A Better Sailor   Page 51

Chapter 5
Distance of the Horizon — Page 55
Distance of the Horizon Answers — Page 63

Chapter 6
Heavy Weather Sailing — Page 65

Chapter 7
Bow & Beam Bearings — Page 71
Bow & Beam Bearings Answers — Page 78

Chapter 8
Learn to Maneuver Your Boat — Page 85

Chapter 9
Chart Reading — Page 89

Chapter 10
Plotting — Page 95
Plotting Answers — Page 108

Chapter 11
Follow Your Navigational Plan — Page 113

Chapter 12
Fear, Remembranc,e and Reality — Page 117

Sailing Terms Spoken Every Day — Page 123

PART TWO
CELESTIAL NAVIGATION

Introduction — Page 127

Chapter 13
The Sextant — Page 131

Chapter 14
The Nautical Almanac — Page 149

Chapter 15
GP The Daily Pages — Page 157

Chapter 16
LHA — Page 165

Chapter 17
Stars & Planets — Page 185

Chapter 18
Star Finders — Page 195

Chapter 19
The Moon — Page 199

Chapter 20
The Noon Sight — Page 201

Captain Jack's Complete Navigation, By Jack I. Davis

Boating Stories   Page 209

    Preface   Page 211

    Rigging Problems   Page 213

    Isla Mujeres, Mexico   Page 219

    The Making Of A Fisherman   Page 223

    Centerboard Nightmare   Page 229

    Clean Fuel   Page 237

    "Come Back" Little Texaco   Page 243

About The Author   Page 255

Captain Jack's Complete Navigation, By Jack I. Davis

PART ONE

BASIC

NAVIGATION

INTRODUCTION

I have about 30,000 blue water sailing miles behind me plus another 5,000 blue water power boat miles. Add to that 5,000 very boring Intracoastal waterway miles and some 1,000 three or four hour sailing lessons and you can see I've spent a lot of time on boats. Most of this time has been thoroughly enjoyable.

Some of the less joyful things are storms. Storms at sea are not much fun and storms lasting for weeks at a time are not much fun for weeks at a time. We have to take the bad with the good.

When I first started to teach sailing courses, I was surprised at the satisfaction I derived from the experience. For me, there is a sense of accomplishment which didn't exist in many of my other endeavors.

After going through the basics of sailing, many of my sailing students wanted to further improve their knowledge of the sea. This led me into teaching my first navigation classes.

Teaching these navigation classes was satisfying, but frustration began when I could not get through to many of the students. I learned that most of these slow students weren't slow at all. They just had an inept instructor. ME!

By refining my techniques and borrowing ideas from others, I found I had fewer and fewer slow students.

Captain Jack's Complete Navigation, By Jack I. Davis

This book utilizes the same techniques as a method for the reader to become a competent navigator.

The format presented here is the classroom presentation. Included is my practice of interspersing many of my sea stories with the real work. Of course, these are the same stories my former students are already more familiar with than they want to be.

Many of my explanations, diagrams and procedures have come about as the most practical way for me to introduce newcomers to the navigational procedures on a boat. They may not reflect absolute scientific explanation but they will teach you what you must know.

I must admit, I've picked up many ideas and techniques from others. Too numerous to mention them all but I do want to acknowledge a few of the main ones.

First, many years ago I took an Intermediate Navigation correspondence course from the University of Tennessee. This was my first and only venture into the academic aspects of navigation. It was a good venture, and in reviewing my teaching methods, I see the influence of that well-structured course.

Second, in preparing for my first U. S. Coast Guard captain's license examination, I reviewed a book by Richard A. Block, published by Marine Education Textbooks. His navigation presentation was by far the best and most comprehensive of any on the market. I know my teaching methods have been greatly affected by Mr. Block's work.

Third, the number one authority on navigation, in my opinion, is Bowditch. I use both Volumes I and II extensively.

Last but not least, I must acknowledge and thank the hundreds of sailors I have sailed with through the years. I have learned something, from nearly every one of them, which influences my teaching and definitely my sea stories.

I want to especially thank Lynn Pinkerton and Sandy Billings for encouraging me to write this book and my first mate, Mary, for spelling and grammar lessons I somehow missed in school. Joe Kolb for artwork and friendship. Mike Sutton my sailboat neighbor, who worked the problems and checked the answers.

Jack I. Davis

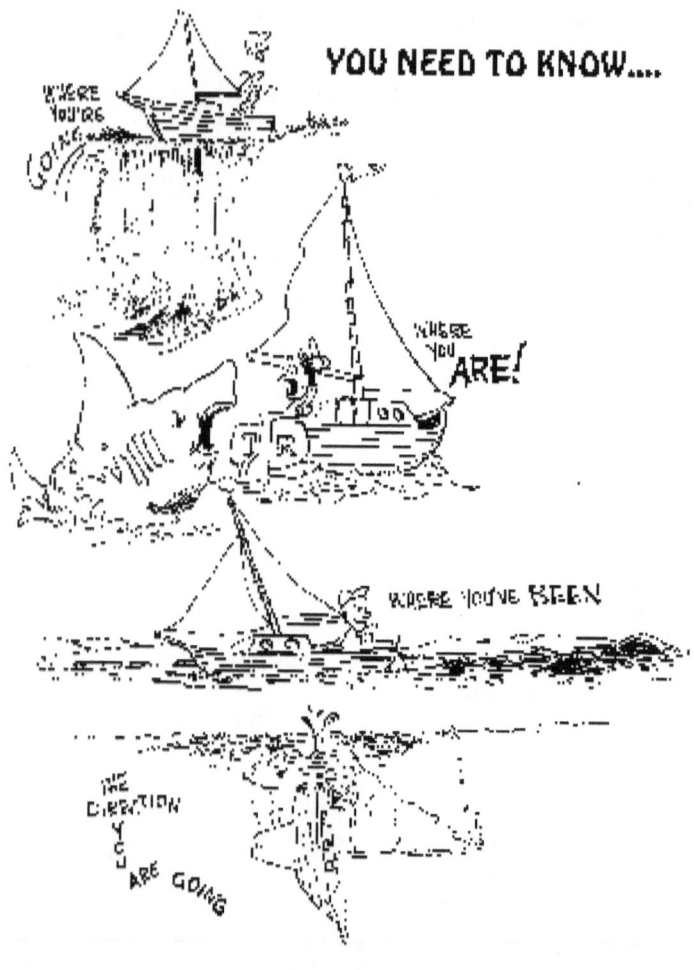

Figure 1

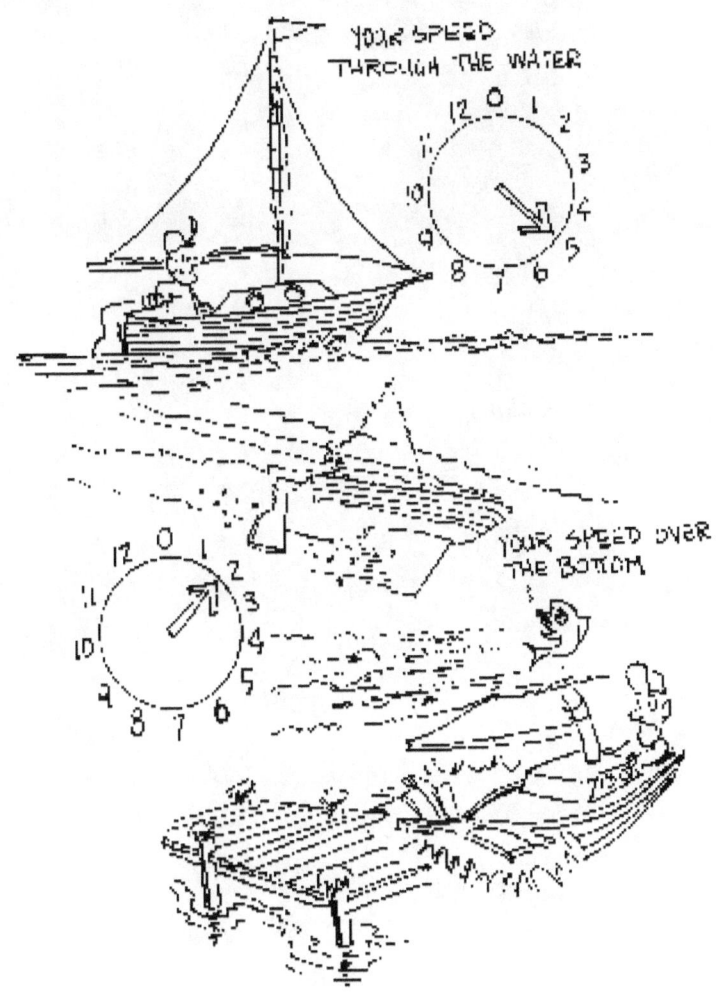

Figure 2

Chapter 1

DISTANCE SPEED AND TIME

Being a good navigator can't be traced to one single skill. It's a composite of many talents.

Today, with the availability of electronic aids, such as GPS (Global Positioning System), you could cross an ocean without the navigational talents in this book. Provided there is no electronic failure.

I see inexperienced people go to sea without the proper abilities. Many make their landfall without major problems but there are some who do have complications. I talked to one of these people and his comment was, "When the electronics failed, it was the most frightening experience of my life. I was not only lost, but I didn't even know where I was before I was lost."

Which brings us to:

Figure 3
Rule # 1 - Always maintain a D. R.

Captain Jack's Complete Navigation, By Jack I. Davis

These letters stand for *Dead Reckoning*. All the time you are under way, keep a record of the course, speed and the elapsed time.

I can not overemphasize the importance of keeping a systematic record of your distance, speed and elapsed time, while at sea. For the electronic sailor who does not maintain a DR, I recommended he glue a mirror just below his GPS or Loran. When the electronics fail, he can then look in the mirror and see who is lost.

In order to plot your course, time and speed onto your chart, you must learn to calculate distance, speed and time.

Don't worry about the difficult calculations. The most complicated math involved in our navigational procedures is elementary math. As simple as it is, you should use your hand held calculator to further simplify checking the answers.

Everyone does a certain amount of these calculations while driving from point A to point B. If these points are 60 miles apart and your car speed is 60 miles per hour, it's going to take an hour to make the trip. You can conclude: You're traveling one mile per minute at 60 miles per hour, in 30 minutes you will be halfway there. Navigation is that simple.

In this case you are solving for distance. You know your speed (60 mph) and the elapsed time (30 minutes). The formula to solve this problem is Distance = Speed x Time. We put down 60 mph for speed and .5 for elapsed time (30 minutes is one half of an hour, or .5). Then 60 times .5 equals 30, or 30 miles, the answer to the problem.

We may also need to solve for speed. This formula is:

S = D / T (The / symbol represents *Divided By*). If we have made 30 miles in 30 minutes (.5 hours) we divide 30 by .5 which equals 60 (mph).

To solve for time, the formula is T = D / S. If we have traveled 30 miles at a speed of 60 mph, we divide the 30 by 60 which equals .5 (.5 hr = 30 minutes)

These formulae are critical. If you use the wrong formula, as is so easy to do, the answer will definitely be wrong. Instead of trying to remember all these formulas there is a better solution.

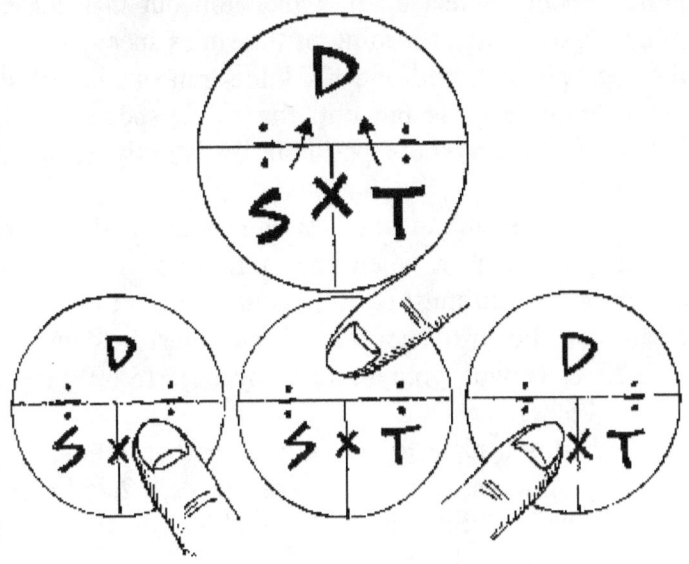

Figure 4

This figure includes all three formulas: To solve for T (time) you divide D by S. To Solve for D (distance) you multiply S times T. To solve for S (speed) you divide D by T.

Please be certain you understand this and do not try to remember the formulas. Always write the formula on the work paper.

In the examples given for distance, speed and time, the examples were mph (miles per hour) and the distances were statue miles, used by most landlubbers. The statue mile is 5,280 feet, but the nautical mile is 6,080 feet.

Everything shown from here on will be nautical miles (nm) and knots (kn). Note, I did not say knots per hour, which is incorrect.

A knot is the speed of 1 nautical mile per hour. Derived from the Common Log where the number of knots (about 25 feet apart) which ran out in a quarter minute gave a direct reading of the ship's speed. Thus, if the log was streamed and six knots ran out before the quarter-minute glass ran out, the ship's speed was six knots. To say 6 knots per hour is, strictly speaking, incorrect.

I use the abbreviation *hr* for hours and *min* for minutes. Remember: when you multiply or divide hours and minutes, you must convert your minutes to fractions of an hour. For instance: 2 hr 15 min must be converted to 2.25 hr (divide your minutes by 60). 15/60 minutes equals .25 hr.

When you have found an answer that is hours and fractions of hours, you must convert it back: 2.25 hr must be converted to 2 hr 15 min (You multiply the fraction by 60). .25 X 60 equals 15 min.

If I am using a hand held calculator, I carry all the decimal places that the gadget will allow me to carry: 2 hr 22 min (22/60 equals .36666666).

If I must use long division or multiplication (with paper and pencil), I round off to .367. The difference will be acceptable.

It is important to work all of the following problems, even if you think you know how to do them. You may be surprised. The answers are at the end of this chapter.

Captain Jack's Complete Navigation, By Jack I. Davis

DISTANCE	SPEED	TIME
1. _____?	7 kn	3 hr
2. _____?	5.5 kn	4 hr
3. _____?	13.5 kn	3.5 hr
4. _____?	17 kn	3 hr 10 min
5. _____?	24 kn	3 hr 10 min
6. _____?	2.7 kn	.8 hr
7. _____?	42.4 kn	16 min
8. _____?	23 kn	46 min
9. 43 nm	6.2 kn	_____?
10. 32 nm	8.5 kn	_____?
11. 35 nm	12.3 kn	_____?
12. 17 nm	28 kn	_____?
13. 15 nm	3.5 kn	_____?
14. 17.8 nm	29 kn	_____?
15. 6.6 nm	19.3 kn	_____?
16. 8.1 nm	16.9 kn	_____?
17. 22 nm	_____?	29 min

18. 23.8 nm _____ ? 0.6 hr

19. 12.3 nm _____ ? 19 min

20. 34 nm   _____ ? 88 min

21. 24.1 nm _____ ? 77 min

22. 16.5 nm _____ ? 0.48 hr

23. 18.9 nm _____ ? 0.77 hr

24. 17.1 nm _____ ? 1.5 hr

In school, the stated problem was one of my least favorite problems. Life, as it turns out, is a stated problem. Certainly, navigation on a small boat is a stated problem. Don't be intimidated. Try to look at each problem as if it is a real life situation and you are the navigator in charge.

25. The distance between two buoys is 14 nm. The vessel's speed is 11 kn. The running time between the two buoys is _____?

26. Your boat's speed is 12 kn. The speed of the current is 3 kn. What is the speed of your boat over the bottom while going upstream against the current _____?

27. Your boat's speed is 12 kn. The current's drift is 2 kn. (The speed of a current is called drift). What is the speed of your boat over the bottom as it travels downstream with the current _____?

28. If you have a 2 kn current and can make 13 kn with a 6 nm run in each direction, how long would it take for a round trip _____?

Be certain to work this problem as two separate legs then add the results together. The answer will surprise most folks.

29. Point "B" is 59 nm from point "A" on a course of 345 degrees true. The current sets 165 degrees true at a drift of 1.7 kn. If your vessel's speed is 12.6 kn, how long will it take you to reach point "B" from point "A" _____?

You already know drift is the speed of the current. Now, here is a new term: Set. Set is the direction the current is going.

30. Your course from "B" to "A" is north on a leg of 10 nm. Your boat's speed is 10 kn. The current's set is 180 degrees with a drift of 4 kn. What is your speed over the bottom _____?

31. Your vessel is making way through the water at a speed of 13 kn. Your vessel traveled 30 nm in 4 hr 23 min. What current are you experiencing _____?

Captain Jack's Complete Navigation, By Jack I. Davis

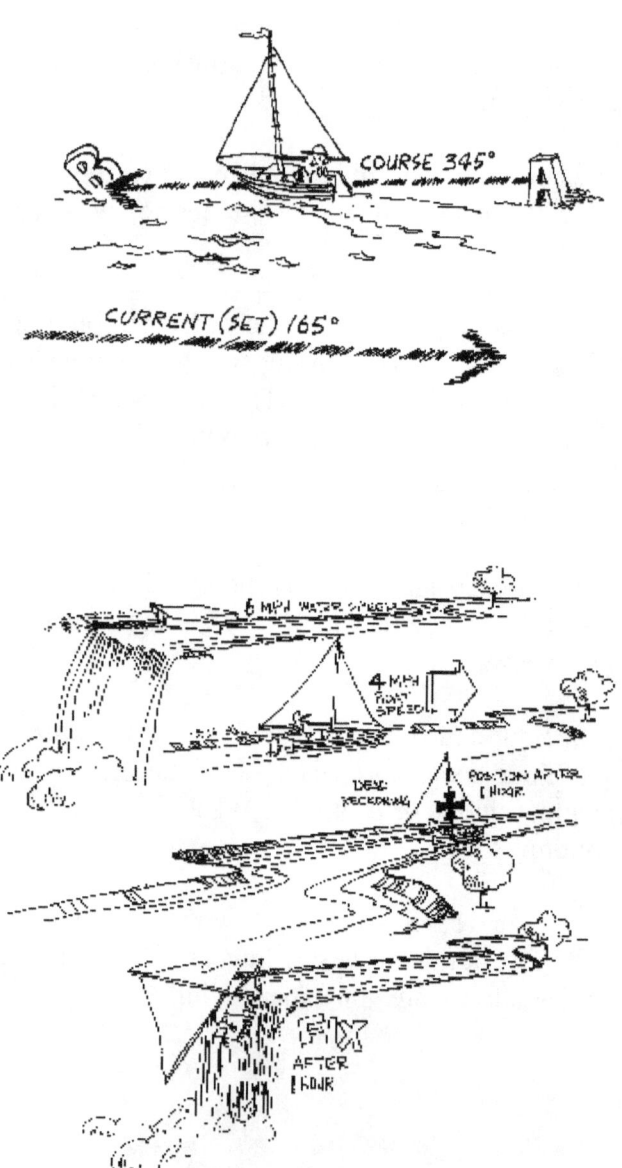

Figure 5, 6 and 7

DISTANCE SPEED TIME ANSWERS

1. 7 kn x 3 hr = 21 nm

2. 5.5 kn x 4 hr = 22 nm

3. 13.5 kn x 3.5 hr = 47.25 nm

4. 17 kn x 3.1666666 = 53.8333 nm

5. 24 kn x 3.16666 hr = 75.9 nm

6. 2.7 kn x .8 hr = 2.16 nm

7. 42.4 kn x .266666 hr = 11.30666 nm

8. 23 kn x .7666666 = 17.6333 nm

9. 43 nm / 6.2 kn = 6.9354838 hr or 6:56 hr & min

10. 32 nm / 8.5 kn = 3.7647058 hr or 3:46 hr & min

11. 35 nm / 12.3 kn = 2.8455284 hr or 2:51 hr & min

12. 17 nm / 28 kn = .6071428 hr or 0:36 min

13. 15 nm / 3.5 kn = 4.2857142 hr or 4:17 hr & min

14. 17.8 nm / 29 kn = .613793 hr or 0:37 min

15. 6.6 nm / 19.3 kn = .341968 hr or 0:21 min

16. 8.1 nm / 16.9 kn = .4792899 hr or 0:29 min

17. 22 nm / .483333 hr = 45.517 kn

18. 23.8 nm / .6 hr = 39.666 kn

19. 12.3 nm / .316666 hr = 38.842 kn

20. 34 nm / 1.4666666 hr = 23.1818 kn

21. 24.1 nm / 1.2833 hr = 18.779 kn

22. 16.5 nm / 0.48 hr = 34.375 kn

23. 18.9 / .77 hr = 24.545 kn

24. 17.1 nm / 1.5 hr = 11.4 kn

25. 14 nm / 11 kn = 1:16 hr & min

26. 12 kn - 3 kn = 9 kn

27. 12 kn + 2 kn = 14 kn

28. Work as two legs:
    1st leg 6 nm - (13 - 2) =   .54545
    2nd leg 6 nm - (13 + 2) =   .40000
                                  .94545 hr

The temptation in this problem is to reason that the current coming and going balances out. Therefore, you could simply use 13 kn = 0:55384 min which will not provide the correct answer.

29. Then:
   59 nm / 10.9 kn = 5.41284 hr
   Then:
   .41284 X 60 = :247706 min = 5 hr 25 min

30. The course - North (360 degrees)
    The current sets South (180 degrees)
    Speed 6 kn

31. 30 nm - 4.383333 hr = 6.844111 kn (Speed made good)   Then:
    Boat speed 13 kn
    less 6.8441111 (speed made good)
    drift 6.155889 (speed of current)

Chapter 2
LEARN TO SAIL

When I bought my first sailboat, the owner went with me on a sea trial which lasted about three hours. That was the extent of my formal sailing education. The balance came in the most difficult way possible, trial and error. In retrospect, it was as much a comedy of errors as a learning experience. I cringe to think of the daily horror stories my little boat and I lived through.

It would have been far better to pay someone to teach me properly, than to get myself beat up so many times. My survival is a true tribute to the strength and integrity of my boat.

Reading the sailing stories of others and their mistakes helped me avoid a few of my own but the better choice would have been lessons.

There are hundreds of charter operators in the nation who offer these lessons and the charge for the course will be money well spent. Of course, some are better than others. Ask for references and check them out carefully before spending your hard-earned money.

There are also Learn to Sail schools and sailing vacation charters with sailing lessons thrown in. I don't like this approach as they seem to throw a lot at their students in a short period of time. Several of my sailing students had been through a concentrated six-day school. They knew less than the students who had been through five lessons of four hours each. The less concentrated course provided the time in between the lessons to absorb the experience.

There are a few sailing school operators who take students out on pleasure cruises. There are refreshments, congeniality and camaraderie, but they impart very little sailing knowledge. I find nothing wrong with people going out to have fun, but I resent those operators referring to their operations as schools.

In most Learn to Sail programs, the student is exposed to different boats and the more the better. You must know the good and the bad attributes of boats before you start on the boat buying trail.

Between the upcoming navigation chapters, there will be further advice and recommendations for the sailors who intend to pursue the cruising life.

Chapter 3
COMPASS

If you draw a line from where you are standing to the North Pole, that direction would be true north. A magnetic compass does not point toward the North Pole, instead it points toward magnetic north.

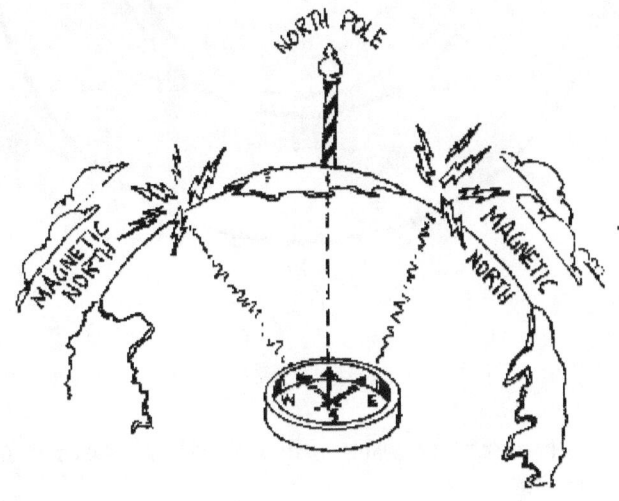

Figure 9

Magnetic north is fairly close to the North Pole but far enough away to cause some major differences. Because of the earth's magnetic pattern, this magnetic north position changes from area to area. This difference between true north and magnetic north is called variation.

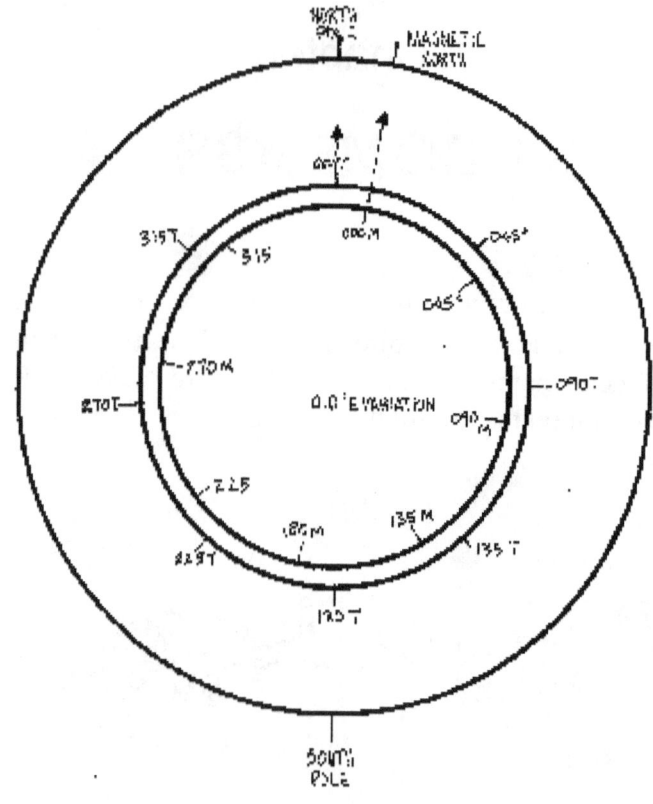

Figure 8

The outer compass rose points toward the North Pole.

When Columbus left the Mediterranean on his expedition to find a shorter route to the far east, he was only familiar with the zero magnetic variation that exists in much of the area between Spain and Italy. The Mediterranean sailors of that time checked their compass against Polaris, the North Star.

The captains and crews of that expedition were shocked to find the farther west they went in the Atlantic, the more their compasses were off in relation to Polaris. We know now that in the mid-Atlantic, the compass variation was as much as twenty degrees, and then it slowly decreases as you move further west. When Columbus made landfall in the Bahamas, the variation was down to two degrees.

All of the charts we use for navigation show the compass variation. This must be taken into consideration in our plotting.

Each of these charts has a compass rose in one or more places on the chart. See figure 8. The compass rose is made up of two parts:

The outer rose, which points toward true north.

The inner rose, which points to magnetic north for that area of the chart.

In the center of the rose the amount of variation and whether the variation is east or west is shown, along with the rate of annual change. This annual change is a very small number and if the charts are fairly recent, the change is of little importance. With very old charts, however, the accumulated annual changes could add up and be a concern, but then again, you shouldn't be using very old charts.

In addition to variation, another situation can affect your ship's compass. All metal on board, either magnetic or nonmagnetic, can move the compass needle. This movement is called deviation.

Deviation on a vessel does not necessarily remain constant. If you move a radio from one location to another, the deviation can change dramatically. This is caused by the magnets used in the construction of the speakers. Occasionally, even canned goods may have an effect, if you put them on board close to the compass.

I spent an hour swinging the compass on a new boat I was to deliver from St. Petersburg to Houston. Later, I noticed a soda can hidden close behind the compass. When I moved it, the compass needle moved fifteen degrees. I then started over and spent another hour swinging the compass.

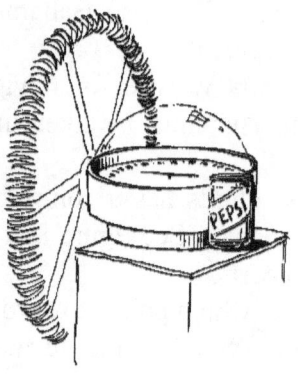

Figure 10

Deviation Card					
Compass	Deviation	Compass	Deviation	Compass	Deviation
000°	001° E	123.7°	005° W	225°	003° W
011.2°	002° E	135°	006° W	236.2°	002° W
022.5°	002° E	146.2°	006° W	247.5°	002° W
033.8°	001° E	157.5°	004° W	258.7°	002° W
045°	001° E	168.7°	004° W	270°	002° W
056.2°	000°	180°	004° W	281.2°	001° W
067.5°	000°	191.2°	003° W	292.5°	001° W
078.8°	002° W	202.5°	003° W	303.7°	000°
090°	003° W	213.7°	003° W	315°	000°
101.2°	004° W	225°	003° W	236.2°	000°
112.5°	005° W	236.2°	003° W	337.5°	001° W
				348.7°	001° W

Table 1 JID

A typical deviation card

You can have your compass swung, by a professional to determine the deviation, or you can learn to do this yourself. In any event, you will then have a deviation card showing the amount of deviation on several headings.

Next, we will present some basic procedures for checking deviation so you can pick up changes which may occur.

With variation and deviation we must have a system, first of all, for correcting the compass:

While sailing let's assume our compass reads 234°
On that heading, our deviation card shows $+005^O$ E
We add the east correction giving us 239°
Our chart shows a variation of $+005^O$ E
We add the east correction giving us 244°
The true course we plot on our chart would be 244°

How can you remember when to add and when to subtract? There is a memory guide for this system as follows:

Compass - we substitute the C in compass   Can
Deviation - we substitute the D in deviation
    Dead
Magnetic - we substitute the M in magnetic   Men
Variation - we substitute the V in variation   Vote
True - we substitute the T in true
    Twice

You can remember "Can dead men vote twice" and add to that AT ELECTION, a reminder to ADD EAST

Many navigators only learn this one system and when they are un-correcting they simply reverse the above procedure, but that can be confusing for most of us. My recommendation is using this un-correcting memory guide:

True - we substitute the T in true	True
Variation - we substitute the V in variation	Virgins
Magnetic - we substitute the M in magnetic	Make
Deviation - we substitute the D in deviation	Dull
Compass - we substitute the C in compass	Companions

We can remember "True virgins make dull companions" and we add to that ADD WHISKEY, to remind us to ADD WEST.

When I sit down at the chart table to plot courses, I put both of these reminders in one corner of my work papers, and the D-S-T symbol in the other. Most of the experienced navigators I've met do the same. It would be risky to work navigation problems off the top of your head.

The following are navigation problems in which you will use your newly learned talents. We will be introducing some words and phrases you will need, so be certain to work all the problems.

1. You desire to make good a course of 090° True. The variation taken from the nearest compass rose on your chart is 005° E. The deviation shown for an easterly heading on your boat's deviation card is 010° W. What course will you steer _____?

The "Course Made Good" shown in figure 11, is what you want to accomplish. There may be a strong current, variation and deviation. The true course from point A to point B is 090°, but you must steer 075° to get there. When you arrive you have made good a course of 090°.

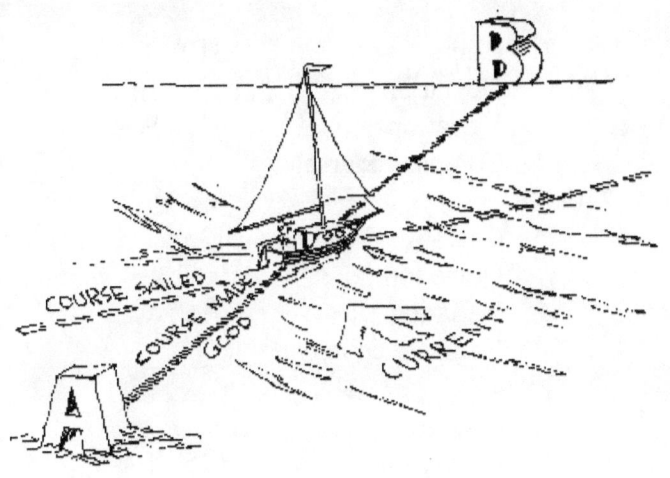

Figure 11

2. The true course you want to make good, as taken from the chart, is 304 . The deviation on this heading is $006°$ E and the variation is $013°$ W. What is the compass course you would steer _____?

3. The true course you want to make good is $276°$. The chart shows the variation in your locality is $012°$ E. The deviation for this heading is $004°$ W. What is the compass course to steer _____?

Many of the errors during these correcting procedures are caused by not lining up the numbers correctly. The neater, the better.

```
T        333°
V        002° W
M        335°  (Always use three digits)
D       + 003° E
C        332°
```

4. Course   310° T
   Deviation   005° E
   Variation   015° W
   Compass course _____?

5. Course   135° T
   Deviation   002° E
   Variation   015° W
   Compass course _____?

6. Course   135° T
   Deviation   006° W
   Variation   012° W
   Compass course _____?

7. Course   020° T
   Deviation   002° E
   Variation   005° W
   Compass course _____?

8. Course   075° T
   Deviation   002° W
   Variation   029° E
   Compass course _____?

9. Course   055° T
   Deviation   007° E
   Variation   014° W
   Compass course _____?

10. Course   150° T
    Deviation   002° E
    Variation   023° W
    Compass course _____?

11. Course   104° T
    Deviation   002° E
    Variation   010° W
    Compass course _____ ?

12. Course   080° T
    Deviation   003° W
    Variation   022° E
    Compass course _____ ?

13. Course   021° T
    Deviation   009° W
    Variation   012° W
    Compass course _____ ?

14. Course   060° T
    Deviation   006° E
    Variation   011° W
    Compass course _____ ?

15. Course   323° T
    Deviation   006° E
    Variation   012° W
    Compass course _____ ?

16. Course   175° T
    Deviation   002° W
    Variation   021° W
    Compass course _____ ?

17. A range is known to be 111° true. You have the ranges in line and directly over the stern. The variation shown on the compass rose is 006°.5` W. If your compass has no deviation, the compass heading should be _____ ?

18. A vessel is heading 270° PSC. On this heading the deviation is 004° W. The variation is 012° E. The true heading is _____? PSC (Per Ship's Compass)

19. A lighthouse bears 237° PSC. Variation is 014° W. Deviation is 001° E. What is the true bearing of the lighthouse _____?

Bearing - The direction from your ship to an object. The bearing of an object is not related to your heading. The bearings of different objects will become increasingly important as we continue.

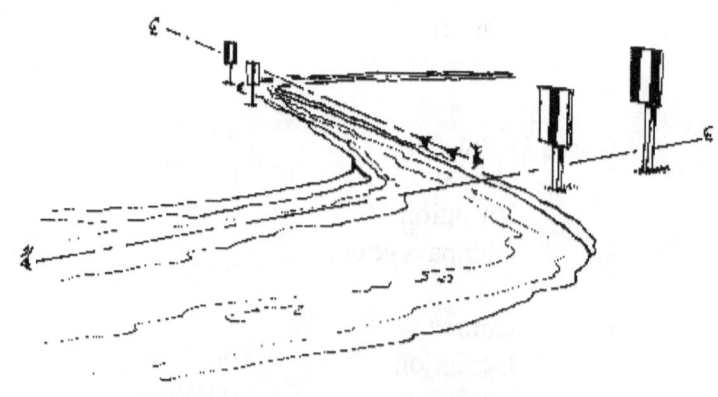

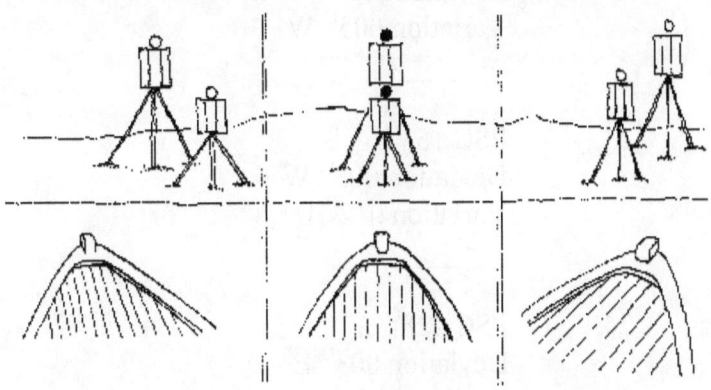

Figure 12

Range markers are used along deep water channels at the bends and turns to give traffic a visual impression of the center of the channel. Looking down the channel, the first range marker you see might be twenty feet tall. The next marker, in line, might be sixty feet tall and one-half mile further down the channel. When you are approaching these markers and have them lined up one above the other, you are precisely in the middle of the channel.

20. PSC 155°
Deviation 004° E
Variation 008° W
_____?

21. PSC 168°
Deviation 006° W
Variation 008° W
_____?

22. PSC 076°

Deviation 000°
Variation 005° W
_____?

23. PSC 153°
Deviation 003° W
Variation 012° E
_____?

24. PSC 228°
Deviation 003° E
Variation 023° E
_____?

25. PSC 120°
Deviation 002°.5` E
Variation 022°.5` E
_____?

26. PSC 071°
Deviation 006° E
Variation 002° W
_____?

27. PSC 034°
Deviation 010° W
Variation 020° W
_____?

28. PSC 081°
Deviation 010° W
Variation 019° E
_____?

29. The bearing of a range taken from the inner circle of the compass rose on a local chart was found to be 177°. The bearing of the same range taken on the boat's compass was 175°. What was the deviation of the compass on that particular boat. _____?

30. Two range lights are in line bearing 054° by compass. The true direction of the range is 049°. Variation according to the chart is 010° W. The deviation of the compass is _____?

31. The deviation of a compass for a 235° compass reading and 232° true course with a variation of 004° E is _____?

32. Three buoys in line bear 062° by the magnetic compass rose on a chart. When parallel with these buoys, your compass reads 058°. What is your deviation on this heading _____?

33.   Magnetic 200°
           Compass 178°
           Deviation _____?

34.   PSC 091°
           True 084°
           Variation 008° W
           Deviation _____?

35.	PSC 015°
	True 010°
	Variation 021° E
	Deviation
	_____ ?

36. A set of ranges is known to be 344° true. You have these ranges in line directly off your beam. The variation shown on your chart is 007°.25` W. If your compass heading is 264°.25`, your deviation should be _____ ?

37.	True course 000°
	Deviation 007° E
	Variation 012° W
	PSC
	_____ ?

38.	True course 360°
	Deviation 016° E
	Variation 016° E
	PSC
	_____ ?

COMPASS ANSWERS

1
T 090°
V 005° E
M 085°
D 010° W
C 095°

2
T 304°
V 013° W
M 317°
D 006° E
C 311°

3
T 276°
V 012° E
M 264°
D 004° W
C 268°

4
T 310°
V 015° W
M 325°
D 005° E
C 320°

5
T 135°
V 015° W
M 150°
D 002° E
C 148°

6
T 135°
V 012° W
M 147°
D 006° W
C 153°

7
T 020°
V 005° W
M 025°
D 002° E
C 023°

8
T 075°
V 029° E
M 046°
D 002° W
C 048°

9
T 055°
V 014° W
M 069°
D 007° E
C 062°

10
T 150°
V 023° W
M 173°
D 002° E
C 171°

11
T 104°
V 010° W
M 114°
D 002° E
C 112°

12
T 080°
V 022° E
M 058°
D 003° W
C 061°

13
T 021°
V 012° W
M 033°
D 009° W
C 042°

14
T 060°
V 011° W
M 071°
D 006° E
C 065°

15
T 323°
V 012° W
M 335°
D 006° E
C 329°

16
T 175°
V 021° W
M 196°
D 002° W
C 198°

17
See
Figure
14

18
C 270°
D 004° W
M 266°
V 012° E
T 278°

19
C 237°
D 001° E
M 238°
V 014° W
T 224°

20
C 155°
D 004° E
M 159°
V 008° W
T 151°

21	22	23	24	25
C $168°$	C $076°$	C $153°$	C $228°$	C $120°$
D $006°$ W	D $000°$	D $003°$ W	D $003°$ E	D $002°.5$ E
M $162°$	M $076°$	M $150°$	M $231°$	M $122°.5$ E
V $008°$ W	V $005°$ W	V $012°$ E	V $023°$ E	V $022°.5'$ E
T $154°$	T $071°$	T $162°$	T $254°$	T $145°$

26	27	28	29	30
C $071°$	C $034°$	C $081°$	C $175°$	C $054°$
D $006°$ E	D $010°$ W	D $010°$ W	D $002°$ E	D $005°$ E
M $077°$	M $024°$	M $071°$	M $177°$	M $059°$
V $002°$ W	V $020°$ W	V $019°$ E	V $000°$	V $010°$ W
T $075°$	T $004°$	T $090°$	T $177°$	T $049°$

31	32	33	34	35
C $235°$	C $058°$	C $178°$	C $091°$	C $015°$
D $007°$ W	D $004°$ E	D $022°$ E	D $001°$ E	D $026°$ W
M $228°$	M $062°$	M $200°$	M $092°$	M $349°$
V $004°$ E	V $000°$	V $000°$	V $008°$ W	V $021°$ E
T $232°$	T $062°$	T $200°$	T $084°$	T $010°$

36	37	38
See Figure 15	T $000°$	T $360°$
	V $012°$ W	V $016°$ E
	M $012°$	M $344°$
	D $007°$ E	D $016°$ E
	C $005°$	C $328°$

Figure 14

Answer for 17. The key phrase is "over the stern!"

111° true
180° reciprocal
291° true boat course - Then   T   291°
                                V   006°.5' W
                                M   297°.5
                                D   000°
                                C   297°.5

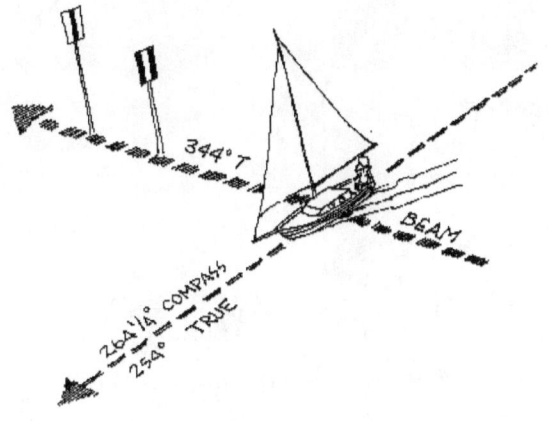

Figure 15

Answer to 36. Beam is a hypothetical line at a 90° angle to keel. If you were going north, the beam would run east and west.

344°	C	264°.25
-90° Beam	D	003° W
254°	M	261°.25
	V	007°.25 W
	T	254°

Chapter 4

TO BE A BETTER SAILOR

There are sailors and then there are sailors. As with any endeavor, the more time and effort you put into it, the better and more proficient you become.

In most sports, like golf or bowling, the person who spends the most time practicing is usually the better athlete.

With sailing, practice helps, to a point. When something happens that you have not practiced, or even contemplated, you may be in trouble. You must know what you are going to do in any situation that could arise, even though you have never practiced the procedure.

There is no way to prepare for every eventuality, but you can read the stories of the hundreds of sailors who have gone before you. You can read about their storms, their groundings, what someone did when the mast fell, the sails blew out or their water supply became contaminated.

In one of Erick Hiscock's stories, he explains sailing off the anchor, which at that time had not occurred to me. He was in a remote anchorage in the South Pacific and when he was ready to leave, the engine would not start.

He described his tactic of raising the main and tacking back and forth until he sailed across the anchor, at which time he could break it loose and continue on.

With his book open to that passage, I took my boat out and dropped anchor. Following his instructions, I sailed off the anchor. That maneuver then became a standard part of my sailing instructions and I always try to relate the story of how I learned it.

I have read about the "Hove To" maneuver, not only in the Hiscock books, but in many other stories by circumnavigators. I was well convinced of the viability of the tactic before I ever tried it.

There are tactics and procedures in stories that I do not agree with, usually because another writer or circumstance has convinced me otherwise. A good example is the sea anchor. There are sailors who swear by the sea anchor and others who swear at them. Certainly the folks who manufacture and sell sea anchors laud them to high heaven, but there are other opinions I respect more.

When I thought of the sea anchor controversy, I had to look carefully at both sides of the debate. Then with my own experiences added to the mix, I was convinced that I would never allow a sea anchor aboard my vessel.

I could rehash this debate but I would only be covering well trotted ground. I suggest reading all you can find on the issue to form your own opinion.

This kind of debate is the exception and not the rule in sailing. Sailing goes far back into history and although there have been some changes through the years, in reality, not much has changed. Most tactics were old hat to sailors hundreds of years ago and therefore there is a proper way to do most everything on a sailboat.

In addition to the Hiscocks, another couple have written several books about their sailing adventures, Len and Larry Pardee. They advocate going small, going inexpensive and going now! Although I don't agree with their Spartan sailing lifestyle, there is much to be said for smaller boats.

There are other books that are not as much fun to read but which you should study; *Chapman's Navigation & Small Boat Handling* is one. I have had a copy aboard for many years and still refer to it often. *Annapolis Book of Seamanship* is another.

You should have a copy of the *United States Coast Pilot #5*. This is a government publication covering a multitude of information not shown on charts or elsewhere.

If you really get serious about your nautical education, you should have *Dutton's Navigation & Piloting* and *Bowditch's American Practical Navigator, Volumes I and II*. I would only recommend *Bowditch's American Practical Navigator, Volume II* for the tables it includes until you have a considerable amount of experience. Until that time, these books have a tendency to tell you more than you need to know.

In my case, I have too many books. Two or three more and my boat may sink and this is a problem for most long-term cruisers. You want to have books aboard to cover everything, but this cannot be.

Chapter 5

DISTANCE OF THE HORIZON

Most of the dangerous navigational problems come about when land is either in sight or some object on land is in sight. I am asked repeatedly, "Are you frightened at being in the middle of the ocean?" The answer, of course, is no. I start to become uneasy (if not frightened) when I get close to land.

When you are sailing in the middle of an ocean or far away from land, there is very little that can do you harm. Close to land there are many things that can do you in; rocks or coral heads, for instance.

One of the important navigational talents is to see a tall object on land and determine how far away it is. The earth is a big round ball with the surface curvature symmetrical. When you are sitting on a boat with your eye level at seven feet above the water, the horizon is always 3.1 nautical miles away.

The following is the mathematical formula that gives us the information in Table 2. This formula is calculating for distance in nautical miles.

Distance = 1.17 x the square root of the height of eye.

As an example: If the height of the eye is 10 feet.

The square root of 10 is 3.1622776. Multiply this figure by 1.17 and the result is the distance to the *horizon* or 3.6998648 which you would round off to 3.7 nautical miles.

The second part of the formula is the same only this time the height of the object is substituted for the height of eye.

Distance = 1.17 x the square root of the height of the object.

As an example: If the height of the object is 30 feet.

The square root of 30 is 5.4772255. Multiply this figure by 1.17 and the result is 6.4083539 which you would round off to 6.4.

3.7 = 1.17 x the square root of the 10.

6.4 = 1.17 x the square root of the 30. Add the two distance answers (3.7 nm) + (6.4 nm) and the sum (10.1 nm) will equal the distance off the object when it is first sighted.

You can use Table 2 as a quick reference. The distances in the table have been calculated for distance away for both height of eye and height of objects.

The table and the formula will provide accurate answers only when the sea is completely flat. Riding the crest of a wave will effect the distances as will being in the trough of a wave. Furthermore, for your safety, never assume the table or the formula will provide more than an approximation of the actual distance. ☐

All nautical charts showing the approaches to land show the height of most significant objects along the shore. The Coast Guard has another publication called the *Light List* which shows the height of all aids to navigation, such as range markers, light towers and the luminous range of a light atop the object.

Luminous Range - The distance the object may be seen on a clear night without regard to curvature of the earth. The light may be bright enough to be seen 25 miles away but at that distance it would be below the horizon. Inversely, the object is high enough to be seen 25 miles away but the light only has a luminous range of 10 miles.

DISTANCE OF THE HORIZON

Height Feet	Nautical Miles	Statute Miles	Height Feet	Nautical Miles	Statute Miles
1	1.2	1.3	38	7.2	8.3
2	1.7	1.9	39	7.3	8.4
3	2	2.3	40	7.4	8.5
4	2.3	2.7	41	7.5	8.6
5	2.6	3	42	7.6	8.7
6	2.9	3.3	43	7.7	8.8
7	3.1	3.6	44	7.8	8.9
8	3.3	3.8	45	7.8	9
9	3.5	4	46	7.9	9.1
10	3.7	4.3	47	8	9.2
11	3.9	4.5	48	8.1	9.3
12	4.1	4.7	49	8.2	9.4
13	4.2	4.9	50	8.3	9.5
14	4.4	5	55	8.7	10
15	4.5	5.2	60	9.1	10.4
16	4.7	5.4	65	9.4	10.9
17	4.8	5.6	70	9.8	11.3
18	5	5.7	75	10.1	11.7
19	5.1	5.9	80	10.5	12
20	5.2	6	85	10.8	12.4
21	5.4	6.2	90	11.1	12.8
22	5.5	6.3	95	11.4	13.1
2	5.6	6.5	100	11.7	13.5
Height Feet	Nautical Miles	Statute Miles	Height Feet	Nautical Miles	Statute Miles
24	5.7	6.6	105	12	13.8

Captain Jack's Complete Navigation, By Jack I. Davis

25	5.9	6.7	110	12.3	14.1
26	6	6.9	115	12.5	14.4
27	6.1	7	120	12.8	14.7
28	6.2	7.1	125	13.1	15.1
29	6.3	7.4	130	13.3	15.4
30	6.4	7.5	135	13.6	15.6
31	6.5	7.6	140	13.8	15.9
32	6.6	7.7	145	14.1	16.2
33	6.7	7.9	150	14.3	16.5
34	6.8	8	160	14.8	17
35	6.9	8.1	170	15.3	17.6
36	7	8.2	180	15.7	18.1

Table 2 BFP

Only <u>distances</u> can be added or subtracted in Table 2. Never add or subtract heights. If your height of eye is ten feet (3.7 nm) and the height of an object is 20 feet (5.2 nm), you add the distances together and they equal 8.9 miles, which is correct. If you were to add the two heights together to total 30 feet, the answer would be 6.4 miles, which is wrong.

Many times at sea with students aboard, I have demonstrated "Bobbing The Light". This occurs when we are nearing a landfall and we know an object of a certain height with a light on top is near our landfall. When we first spot the light, we can be reasonably sure of our distance away using the formula or table. To double check your answer, you sit down and the light will go out of sight. When you stand up the light is in sight, thus "Bobbing The Light". See figures 16 and 16a.

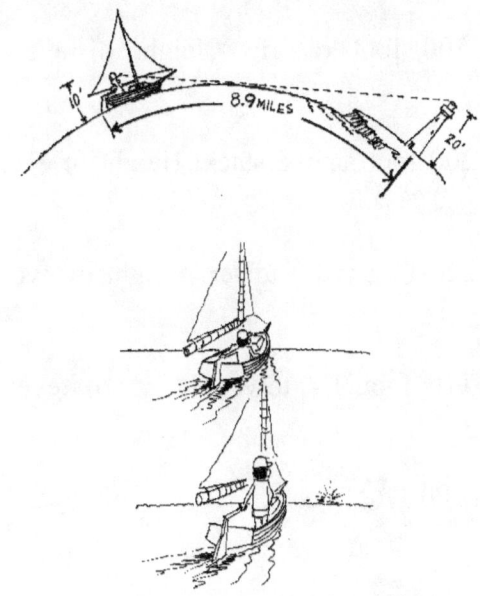

Figures 16 and 16a

Standing, the light is visible. Sitting it is not.

The following problems will give you an opportunity to be certain you understand the proper methods for using the table and the formula. You will notice some questions use a height that is not in the table. You must use the formula or a combination of the formula and the table to achieve the correct answer for these questions. The answers are at the end of the chapter.

1. You sight a 780 foot mountain peak just clearing the horizon. If your height of eye is 15 feet, what is your distance away _____?

2. Assuming good visibility, how far is each light visible for the height of eye shown.

a. 300 foot oil rig. Height of eye: 20 feet. _____ ?

b. 200 foot smoke stack. Height of eye: 60 feet. _____ ?

c. 220 foot radio tower. Height of eye: 12 feet. _____ ?

d. 110 foot TV tower. Height of eye: 12 feet. _____ ?

e. 200 foot tank. Height of eye: 10 feet. _____ ?

3. A navigational light 120 feet above sea level has a charted range of 20 miles. What must your height of eye be to see this light at its charted range _____ ?

4. A light 115 feet high to an observer at sea level compared to a light 100 feet high to an observer with a height of eye of 15 feet _____ ?

5. On a clear dark night, you identify a light just breaking clear of the horizon. The light is 75 feet high with a charted range of 20 nm. Your height of eye is 50 feet. What is your distance from the light _____ ?

6. A lookout with a height of eye of 55 feet observes a flashing light on the horizon. The light is timed and identified as a navigational light 117 feet above sea level. How far was the vessel from the light when first observed _____ ?

7. To what distance does the sea horizon extend if your height of eye is 8 feet _____?

8. What is the horizon distance for each of the heights:

    a. 34 feet _____?

    b. 115 feet _____?

    c. 180 feet _____?

9. At what distance should you be able to see each of these strong lights:

HEIGHT OF LIGHT	HEIGHT OF EYE	
a. 150 feet	30 feet	?
b. 110 feet	80 feet	?
c. 300 feet	30 feet	?
d. 540 feet	40 feet	?
e. 720 feet	45 feet	?

10. At what distance can you see a light whose height is 150 feet, and charted range is 19 nm? Your height of eye is 42 feet. _____?

DISTANCE OF THE HORIZON ANSWERS

1. 32.7 + 4.5 = 37.2 nm

2.
   a. 20.3 + 5.2 = 25.5 nm

   b. 16.5 + 9.1 = 25.6 nm

   c. 17.4 + 4.1 = 21.5 nm

   d. 12.3 + 4.1 = 16.4 nm

   e. 16.5 + 3.7 = 20.2 nm

3. 12.8 + x = 20, x = 7.2 i.e. height of eye of 38 feet.

4. 11.7 + 4.5 = 16.2
          - 12.5
            3.7

5. 10.1 + 8.3 = 18.4 nm (which is less than charted range)

6. 115'   12.5
    55'   8.7
     2'   1.7
          22.9 nm

This is one of the situations where using the table correctly provides the wrong answer. Mathematical tables are not infallible. Adding the additional 2 feet of height to the light to equal 117 (the table shows 115 and 120) produces a quirk. Obviously you can not be farther off using a light of 117 feet than you would be using a light of 120 feet but using the table correctly shows you are by 1.56 nm. When in doubt, use the next lower number (in this case, 115 feet) in the table in place of adding numbers to achieve a number which is not listed. You could also use the formula, discussed earlier, to achieve the correct answer of 21.34 nautical miles off.

7. 8.0 = 3.3 nm

8.
   a. 34 feet = 6.8

   b. 115 feet = 12.5

   c. 180 feet = 15.7

9.
   a. 20.7

   b. 22.8

   c. 26.7

   d. 34.6

   e. 39.2

10. 150' = 14.3
    42' = 7.6
        21.9 but the Luminous range is 19 nm.

Chapter 6

HEAVY WEATHER SAILING

A well found sailing vessel with an experienced crew can handle almost anything that comes down upon it. I don't want to dwell on the frightening aspects of an otherwise extremely pleasant experience, but there are some things you should know.

There are numerous books available on storm tending and I recommend you read several to expose yourself to different opinions. But let me give you my storm tending philosophy by first relating a story.

Several years ago, an English cruising couple by the name of Erick and Susan Hiscock were sailing down the east coast of the United States after having sailed around the world several times. By this time they had become the most famous cruising couple in the world.

They had written many excellent books about their adventures and numerous articles about sailing for sailing magazines. A yacht club in the Miami area heard they were nearby, hunted them down, and invited them to come in and give a talk for the club's membership.

This they did and upon arriving at the club, Erick asked the master of ceremonies what topic he and Susan should discuss. "How about Heavy Weather Sailing," the emcee said. "But Sir," Erick replied, "Susan and I do not sail in heavy weather."

Which brings me to my point. The Hiscocks watched the seasonal weather very closely and were not about to be caught in a major weather system, except in the rarest of circumstances. In those very rare cases where they were intercepted by violent weather they simply hove-to. In this maneuver, if under sail, you bring your vessel through the wind as if you were going to tack, but without bringing the jib across. After the bow passes through the wind and the jib is back-winded, you then turn the helm all the way over toward the back-winded jib.

Figure 29

Hove-To

When Hove-To, the wind is from the starboard side. The helm is turned to make a starboard turn. The jib sheet remains on the starboard side.

The boat, at that point, is trying to sail into the back-winded jib. It reaches a point of equilibrium and, in effect, is stopped except for a slight amount of leeway.

You can do this with main and jib in winds of forty knots. In heavier winds, you drop the sails, turn the helm hard over and lock it down. You are effectively hove-to, under bare poles.

Several of the most distinguished and capable sailors in the world have used this technique and have written about it. I personally have used it hundreds of times.

On one delivery, I was bringing a new thirty-nine foot Beneteau from Pensacola to Galveston. The vessel had one 130 jib and a standard main without reef points. Normally, I would not have gone to sea without better sail resources but it was a short trip and my better judgment failed me.

About fourteen hours after rounding the Mississippi Delta, on a northwesterly course, we were hit by a winter weather front with winds building to about fifty knots. We dropped the jib and tried to continue with the main alone, but we were overpowered.

We dropped and secured the main, turned the helm hard over and locked it down. We also secured the wheel with a line to be certain the wheel brake didn't slip. We laid ahull for twenty-seven hours with the winds of fifty knots gusting to sixty knots.

After the winds began to let up, we checked our position and found we had been pushed south twenty-four miles in the twenty-seven hours we were hove-to. This meant our leeway was less than one knot. Although it wasn't a pleasant experience, there was no damage to the boat and the crew could rest in between drinking coffee and playing gin.

I could tell hove-to stories for the next hundred pages but let me end with one more story.

I was called into a charter company as a visiting instructor. The concept was a corporation team building exercise of learning to sail. There were groups of four students and one instructor on each of ten different boats. Each group was more or less competing with the other groups.

Prior to the beginning of this exercise, the ten captains had a meeting with the charter operator to discuss plans. They covered starting time, return time and the schedule; two hours of tacking and jibing, anchor drill, etc. I brought up the suggestion of showing the students the hove-to maneuver which I consider to be the most important lesson in sailing. To my great surprise, the other nine instructors didn't teach the maneuver and I don't think many of them understood the concept.

When you take sailing lessons, be certain this maneuver is included, or go out and try it for yourself.

In previous chapters I mentioned my dislike of sea anchors and I will say it again: I don't like or use sea anchors or warps.

In theory, a sea-anchor attached to the bow in storm conditions will hold the bow into the wind, giving the vessel a better ride. The error in this thinking is that a sailboat attached to a sea anchor (or anchor for that matter) will stay straight into the wind. It just doesn't happen.

The main problem is the tremendous forces the sea anchor puts on the boat, so much so that cleats can be torn out and other gear damaged.

The bottom line is that a vessel hove-to will ride better, safer and with less potential damage than a vessel attached to a sea anchor. Provided land is not nearby to leeward, I feel this is the safest method to use when riding out a storm.

I saw a sailboat that had been tied to an offshore drilling platform's mooring buoy during a fifty knot blow. The owner's thinking was that the mooring buoy would hold his bow into the wind (like a sea-anchor), and would be a safe place to ride out the storm. The vessel was virtually destroyed and was ultimately considered a complete loss by the insurance company.

Warps are lines strung behind your boat to help reduce your speed when your running off before a storm. My first question is why run off before a storm? If the storm is that violent, why not hove-to? If there is some logical reason to run down wind in heavy weather, then running without the warps is much safer. There have been several cases of boats pitchpoling when running off trailing warps.

The real keys to handling weather at sea are to have a good inventory of sails and storm sails, know when to use them and have a plan for whatever conditions you might encounter.

Chapter 7

BOW AND BEAM BEARINGS

Distances at sea and along the coast are eminently hard to judge. Like the *Distance of the Horizon* procedure we discussed earlier, it is very helpful to have a tool to determine our distance from an object we are either passing at sea or along the shore.

If we are passing an object, like a drilling platform that is not directly on our course, we can obtain a close approximation of the distance to that object, when we are abeam.

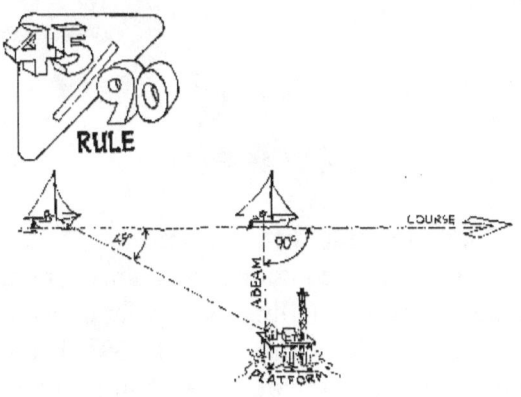

Figure 17
45/90 Rule
Distance Run Equals Distance Abeam

The distance run between 1st and 2nd bearings will be the distance off when abeam. This means, while you are passing an object at sea and it is noted to be forty-five degrees off the bow at one point, and ninety degrees off the bow at another point, then the distance you traveled between the first point and the second point is the distance you are away from the object when you reach the second point.

Figure 17 gives you an example of the 45/90 rule. Thinking back to your high school geometry days, what is described is an isosceles right triangle.

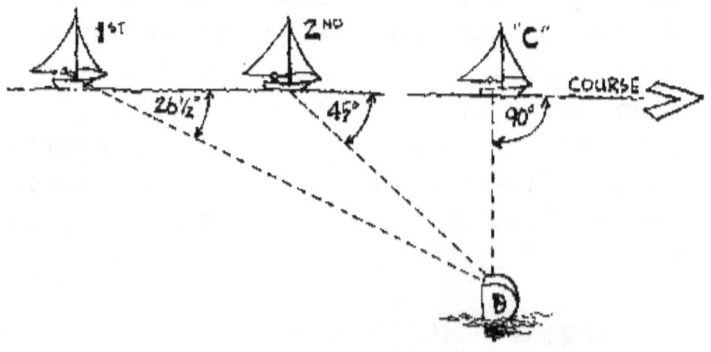

Figure 18

26.5 / 45 Rule

The $26.5°/45°$ rule differs from the $45°/90°$ rule in that it is making a prediction about an event that will occur in the future. It is telling us how far away an object will be long before the object is abeam. This conceivably, could alert you to a change of course, if when abeam, you will be closer to the object than you will want to be.

Double The Angle On The Bow

The Distance Run Is The Distance Off At The Time Of The Second Bearing

This rule basically falls into the same category as the 45/90 rule even though I show it separately. When you take any bearing angle (Not compass heading) and then later take a second bearing that is double the first, the distance run from the first bearing to the second bearing is the distance off at the second bearing.

As an example. You are on a compass heading of 010°. You see a light at a bearing of 055° (45° off the bow) You continue on the 010° compass course until the compass bearing of the light is 100° (90° off the bow) You have doubled the angle on the bow between the 055° reading and the 100° reading. The distance you run during that time is the distance away from the light at the time of the second reading.

One more bearing that you must learn is the bearing to another boat approaching your vessel from port or starboard. Using this procedure correctly will tell you if the oncoming boat will pass in front of your boat, behind your boat or pass right through the saloon of your boat. The steps are as follows.

While maintaining a constant compass course, take a relative bearing of the other boat.

If the relative bearing moves toward the bow, the boat will pass ahead of you.

If the relative bearing moves toward the stern, the boat will pass behind you.

If the relative bearing remains the same, you are about to have guests for dinner!

The above will only give a true answer if the other boat has maintained a constant compass course as well.

Any deviation in the path of either boat will render the process useless.

Now for some problems to test your understanding of Bow and Beam Bearings.

1. You take a bearing of a light house that is $45°$ off the bow and again when it is abeam. The distance run between the two bearings is 4 nm. How far are you off the lighthouse when abeam _____?

2. At 1020 hours a vessel making 15 kn sighted a light bearing $45°$ on the port bow. The light was abeam at 1105 hours and was how far off _____?

3. A vessel proceeding on a course of $000°$ at a speed of 12 kn observes a light bearing $045°$ from the bow at 1015 hours. At 1130 hours the light is abeam and is how far off _____?

4. A light bears $45°$ off the bow at 1000 hours and is abeam at 1045 hours. Your boat's speed is 12 kn. What is your distance off the light at 1045 hours _____?

5. Running at 12 knots, a light bears $45°$ off the bow at 1955 hours and is abeam at 2105. How far off the light are you when abeam _____?

6. A vessel on a course of $090°$ at 12 kn, takes a bearing on a lighthouse at $135°$, and 10 minutes later at $180°$. How far away is the lighthouse at the time of the second bearing _____?

7. You steer $000°$ T at 14 kn in a current setting $180°$ T at a drift of 2 kn. You run 20 minutes between a

bow and beam bearing on a light. How far are you off the light when abeam _____?

8. A vessel sights a light bearing $045°$ off the bow. Holding her course, she travels 5 nm until the light bears $090°$ off the port bow. How far is the vessel off the light at the time of the second bearing _____?

9. A vessel on course $195°$ passes light "A" abeam to starboard at 1427 hours. At 1542 hours buoy "B" bears $150°$ and at 1551 hours is passed abeam to port. The distance from abeam light "A" to abeam buoy "B" is 22.4 nm. The distance off buoy "B" when abeam was _____?
Draw a diagram, plotting all the facts of the problem. This will help solve the problem.

10. At 1010 hours a lighthouse bore $26.5°$ off the bow and 1022 hours it bore $045°$ off the bow. The vessel is making 10 kn, with no current. The vessel's distance from the lighthouse when abeam will be _____? ($26.5°/45°$ Rule)

11. The speed of a boat is 8 kn. A lighthouse is $26.5°$ off the bow at 1000 hours and $45°$ at 1030 hours. When it is abeam, the lighthouse will be how far off _____?

12. The first bearing is a shore light that was $26.5°$ on the starboard bow at 1900 hours. At 1940 hours, a second bearing of $45°$ on the starboard bow was taken. Speed is 15 kn. The light will be abeam at _____? and will be how many miles off _____?

13. A vessel sights a light bearing $26.5°$ off the port bow. Holding her course she travels 5 nm. The light

bears 45° off the port bow. How far will the vessel be off the light when the light is abeam, if she holds her course and speed _____?

14. A vessel sights a light 25° off the starboard bow. She holds course and travels 5 nm when the light bears 50° of her starboard bow. How far is the vessel off the light at the time of the second bearing _____? Double the angle on the bow.

15. A vessel is on course 185° true, speed 10 kn. A light is observed bearing 155° true at 1020 hours. At 1105 hours the light bears 125° true. The distance off at 1105 hours is _____?

16. You are underway at 12 kn with no current or leeway. You see a lighthouse and take a bearing at 1130 hours of 28° off the port bow. At 1201 hours, you take a second bearing which reads 68° off your port bow. How far off at the second bearing _____? How far off will you be at closest approach _____?

Bowditch Volume II, *Table 7* uses any two bearings to determine the distance off at the second bearing and the prediction of the distance off when abeam. This book is a worthwhile purchase to avoid using the formulas that follow.

You can use the following formulae to calculate the distance off at any angle by solving plane and oblique triangles. This is the only set of formulas in this book which require a scientific calculator and higher math skills.

In a right plane triangle you must substitute only the values representing the basic triangle in the appropriate formulas and solve. It then follows, if a and b are known:

$\tan A = a/b$

triangles:
$B = 90 - A$
$c = a \cos A$

If c and B are given:
$A = 90 - B$
$a = c \sin A$
$\cos A$
$b = c \cos A$

Oblique plane

Law of sines:
$$\frac{a}{\sin A} = \frac{b}{\sin B} = \frac{c}{\sin C}$$

Law of cosines
$a^2 = b^2 + c^2 - 2bc$

The above makes it easy to understand why purchasing Bowditch's Volume II is a good investment.

Captain Jack's Complete Navigation, By Jack I. Davis

BOW AND BEAM ANSWERS

Captain Jack's Complete Navigation, By Jack I. Davis

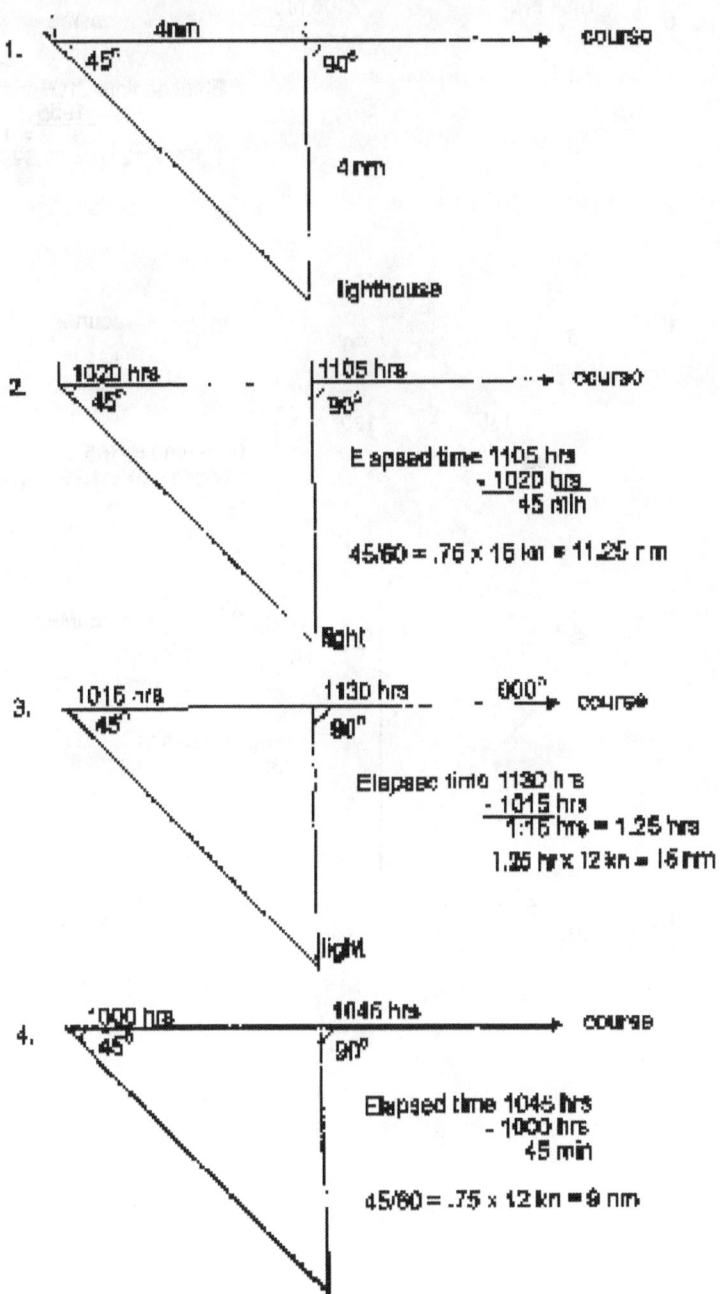

Captain Jack's Complete Navigation, By Jack I. Davis

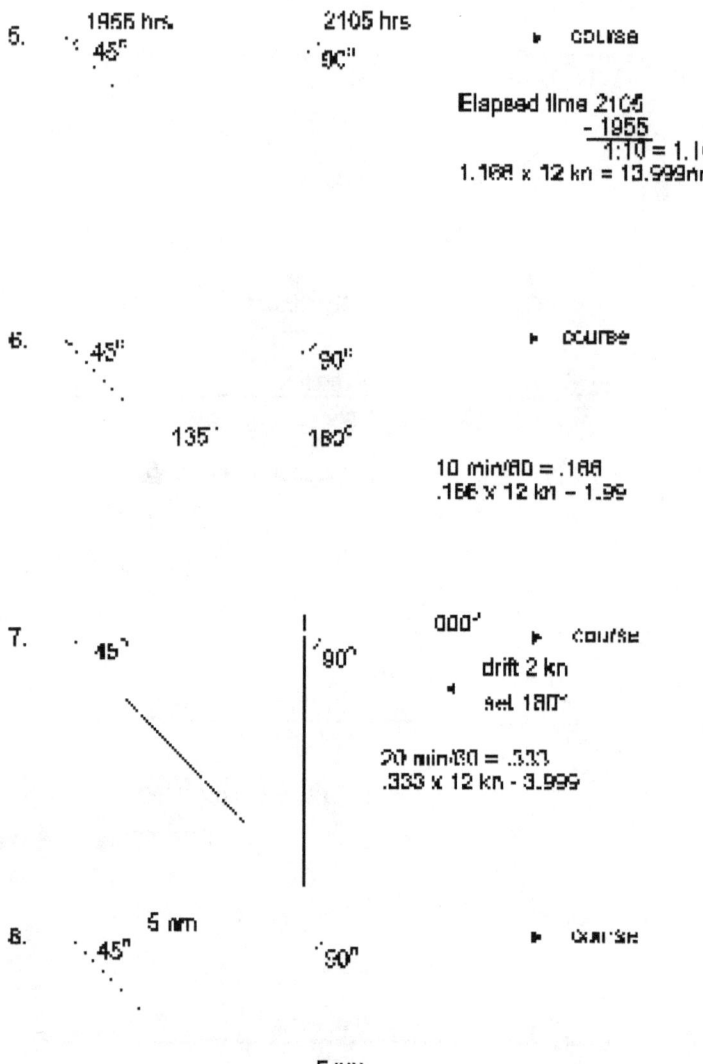

5.   1955 hrs.   2105 hrs
     45°   90°   ► course

                                    Elapsed time 2105
                                              - 1955
                                              1:10 = 1.166
                                    1.166 x 12 kn = 13.999nm

6.   45°   90°   ► course

                135°   180°
                                    10 min/60 = .166
                                    .166 x 12 kn = 1.99

7.   45°   000°   ► course
                         90°   drift 2 kn
                                    set 180°

                                    20 min/60 = .333
                                    .333 x 12 kn = 3.999

8.   5 nm
     45°   90°   ► course

              5 nm

Page 80

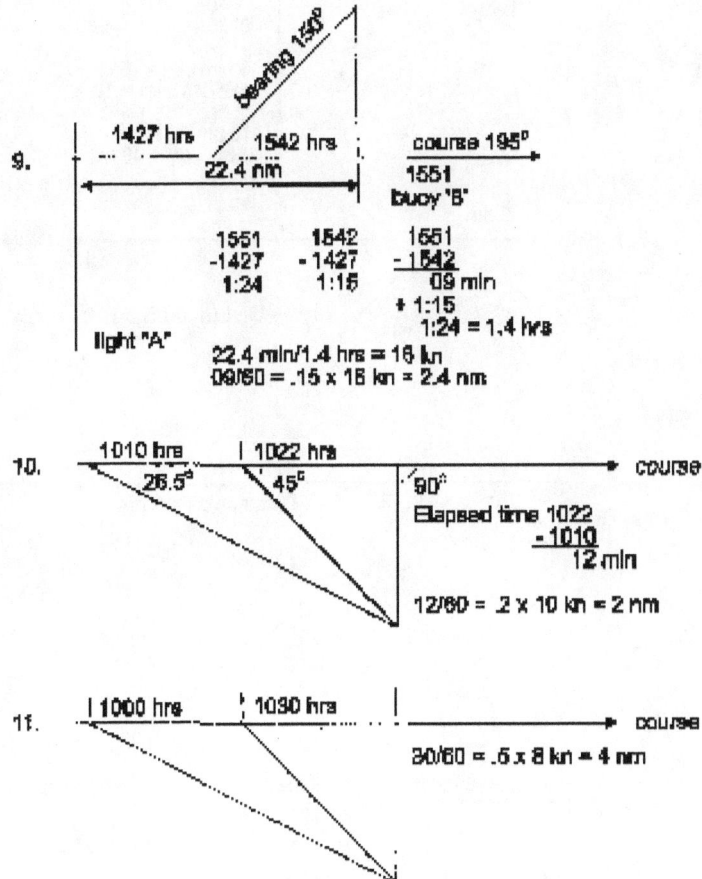

Captain Jack's Complete Navigation, By Jack I. Davis

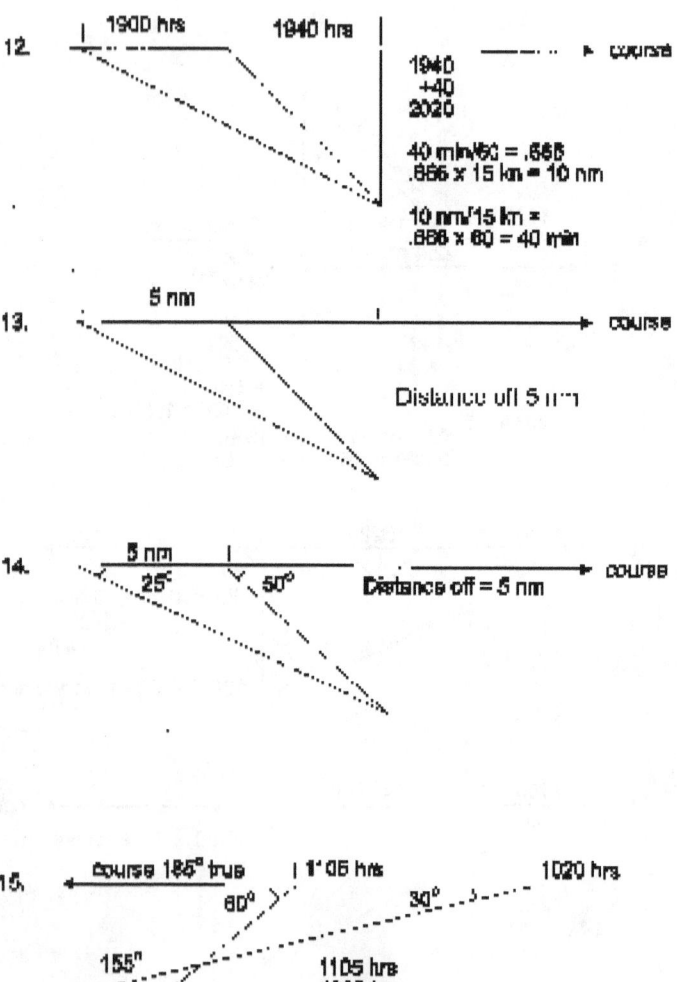

Page 82

Captain Jack's Complete Navigation, By Jack I. Davis

16.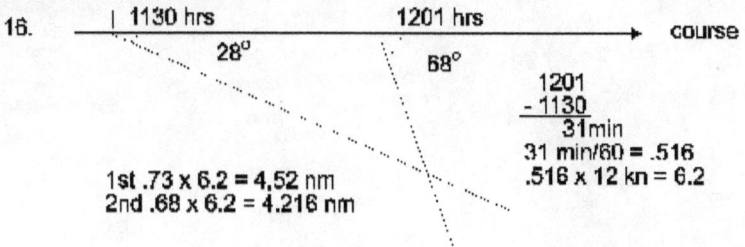

1st .73 x 6.2 = 4.52 nm
2nd .68 x 6.2 = 4.216 nm

1201
- 1130
31min
31 min/60 = .516
.516 x 12 kn = 6.2

Chapter 8

LEARN TO MANEUVER YOUR BOAT

Since most boat damage occurs while docking, leaving the dock or other maneuvers in close quarters, it is imperative to learn how to make your boat do what you want it to do while motoring.

Handling a sailboat, of almost any size, with a single inboard engine is very deceptive when you consider windage, current and the vessel's turning radius. Unfortunately, most newcomers to sailing do not place a high priority on something as mundane as driving around in a sailboat under power.

There are also many long-term sailors who have never learned the ABCs of sailboat maneuvering. Therefore, they get into all kinds of trouble, particularly when wind and current become a factor.

The primary concept in close quarters maneuvering is the effect of torque on your vessel. Your propeller is a screw working its way through the water. Torque is a pulling force, to the side, while your propeller is spinning (prop walk).

In forward gear the force of the prop wash over the rudder gives you control and turning ability and the effect of torque is relatively unimportant. In reverse, there is no rush of water over the rudder and torque will have a tremendous effect.

You can demonstrate this with your boat tied at the dock. Put your engine in reverse at a moderate idle. You will see that, in addition to the backward movement of the boat, there is also a movement to the side, the stern will move to starboard or port. Seventy-five percent of the boats I've been on, the torque in reverse, pulled the stern to port.

When you cast off and start to back out of a slip, the stern of the boat will be pulled to this torque side regardless of what you do with the rudder. Since the prop's wash is forward, there is no water movement over the rudder. The boat speed must reach a point where there is enough water going over the rudder to offset the torque effect, thereby giving some rudder control.

If the torque is to port in reverse, the stern of the boat is going to port. Trying to move the stern to starboard is almost hopeless. You can build speed to gain rudder control, but in many marinas the extra room just doesn't exist.

If you don't have the extra room, let the stern go to port and then make a 270 degree turn, which is easy if you let the torque help.

Back up so your bow clears any pilings, then go to forward gear and accelerate to a moderate idle. Do not turn the helm until you have prop wash over the rudder. (If the boat is moving backward at speed and you turn the helm, the boat will respond to the helm).

When you have forward movement, turn the helm hard over in the direction you want to go. Don't allow excess speed to build. When you reach a fair amount of forward movement, pull the gear shift back into reverse (All sailboat marine gears that I have used are safe to shift at a moderate idle without slowing the engine or stopping in neutral). Remember, the helm is hard over, just leave it alone.

With your boat in reverse, the torque is pulling your stern to the side and helping with your turn. Remain in reverse until the boat is completely stopped. The boat will continue to turn. When you feel the turn slowing and before the boat movement is astern, shift to forward.

If you continue this procedure, the boat will turn, almost on its own axis. It is not unusual for me to have a student turning a thirty-three foot boat in a 45 foot fairway after less than one hour's practice.

If the wind or current is strong, you may need to increase the RPM on your engine to offset the leeway.

Once you understand torque, make it your friend not your enemy.

Captain Jack's Complete Navigation, By Jack I. Davis

Chapter 9
CHART READING

Learning to read a nautical chart is very much like the experience you went through when you saw your first automobile road map. It can be very intimidating to look at all the little squiggles you do not understand. After you learn the basics, the road map is not so intimidating. In fact, it becomes your friend and opens a whole new world for you, allowing you to plan a trip and go almost anywhere.

The nautical chart also is intimidating at first. After you understand the basics it is as easy to use as a road map, and it too opens a new world for you. More so than the road map, because you have fewer limitations.

A nautical chart is a graphic representation on a flat surface, of a navigable portion of the earth's surface. A chart shows the depth of water by numerous soundings, and sometimes by soundings and depth contours, which is a line that joins points of equal depth. This is often shown as a dotted line.

In the lower left or right corners of the chart will be a legend stating how the chart's depths are measured. This may be in fathoms, feet or meters. If you look at a coastal chart giving the depth in fathoms, you may see these dotted lines at the ten, fifty and one hundred fathom areas.

Fathom - A fathom was once considered to be the height of a typical sailor, which at one time was probably about five feet. In more recent times the fathom, by convention, was standardized at six feet.

Marine charts also show the shoreline of adjacent land, topographic features that serve as landmarks, aids to navigation, dangers to navigation and other information of interest to mariners.

You will also find on the chart the fractional scale or chart scale. This can be shown as a representative fraction or as a numerical scale.

In the representative fraction, the scale may be 1:2500. This would be one inch on the chart to 2500 inches in the real world. In other words, if this is a chart of a small bay, one inch on the chart would equal about two hundred and eight feet on the bay.

The 1:2500 chart is known as a large scale chart, as the one inch is large in relation to the 2500 inches. This scale covers a very small area.

A scale of 1:14,000,000 (one inch to 194 miles), is known as a small scale chart and these charts cover a very large area. They are generally used for voyage planning and offshore purposes so you would switch to a larger scale chart (covering a small area) when approaching pilot waters.

Confusing isn't it - the large scale covers the small area and the small scale covers the large area. That's government!

As a general rule, charts will fall into the following categories:

Sailing Charts - These are the smallest scale charts used for planning, and navigating at sea. The Scale on these charts is generally smaller than 1:600,000.

General Charts - These are for coastwise navigation. Their scales range from about 1:150,000 to 1:600,000.

Coastal Charts - Are intended for inshore coastwise navigation where the course may lie inside some reefs and shoals. The scales run from about 1:50,000 to 1:150,000.

Harbor Charts - For navigating in harbors and small waterways. The scales will be larger than 1:50,000.

Most charts will also have a *Graphic Scale*, which is a line or bar graph somewhere on the chart, giving distances in nautical miles, yards, statue miles and/or feet and meters. Instead of using these graphic scales you can use the latitude scale on the side of your chart, since one minute (1') of latitude is equal to one nautical mile.

All of the charts we will be dealing with are *Mercature* charts. This type of chart is an attempt to picture the face of the earth, which is round, on a flat surface. This is much like peeling an orange and trying to get the peels to lay flat. It is, however, the best of several methods to picture this impossible situation. Further in your sailing career, you may have need for other types of charts, such as those used in great circle sailing, or polar charts if you decide to sail around one or both poles.

Chart accuracy - Nautical charts go back a long way, and some of the charts we use go back a long way. I currently use charts of central American waters that are British Admiralty charts from surveys of 1884. Yes 1884! You should always use the most recent charts available and these are it.

The surprising thing to me is that these charts are as accurate as they are, which gives you an indication of how sharp some of those old sailors really were. In relation to current technology they are not up to our space age expectations, but they are better than may be expected.

On the other hand, I had talked to a few NOAA (National Oceanic and Atmospheric Administration) employees returning from a re-surveying trip to central America. They found some of the Admiralty charted islands to be as much as three miles in error.

When considering accuracy of charts, we must consider how accurate they were at the start and what changes may have occurred in the meantime. These changes may be sand drifting, shoaling, reef build up, wrecks or changes in aids to navigation.

The man-made changes, such as aids to navigation, are printed regularly in the Local Notice to Mariners. This is published by each Coast Guard Commander for changes within their District. Offshore changes are published by the Defense Mapping Agency (DMA) and are called Notice to Mariners.

When you buy a new chart, it should incorporate all changes to the date of publication. The chart owner/user is responsible for updating the chart with changes that have occurred since the date of publication. Ask your Coast Guard District Aids to Navigation section to place your name on the mailing list to receive Local Notice to Mariners.

You can obtain (at no cost) a chart catalogue at your local chart store, which will show you the various charts available, their scale and the chart number.

Your most important help in chart reading will come from a publication called *Chart No. 1*. This is jointly prepared by the NOAA (National Oceanic and Atmospheric Administration) and the Department of Defense, Defense Mapping Agency. This is a book (not a chart) showing the meaning of all symbols, abbreviations, terms and wavy lines shown on charts. This too is available at most chart stores or from the government book stores.

Chart water depths may have different meanings based on various data. In general, the charted depths are the least favorable, whether it be mean low water data, mean lower low water data, etc. If your chart shows an area with a depth of eight feet, that would be the worst situation. Under normal conditions you may find the depth to be slightly greater.

Chart heights above the water, for clearance under bridges or power lines, is also a worst case situation but is taken from mean high water soundings.

CAUTION: Power line clearances will state Authorized Clearance. Do not test the limits of power cable clearance. The aluminum mast will provide a wonderful conductor making all aboard a wonderful barbecued feast for the fish.

Chapter 10

PLOTTING

To make the work easier, unfold your plotting sheet and scotch tape the corners to a flat work surface. You will also need a good set of parallel rulers and a set of dividers. As you have probably found, a hand held calculator is also valuable in navigation.

Latitude - These lines are circles around the earth, such as the equator. All latitude lines are parallel to each other and are referred to as parallels of latitude.

You could draw circles of latitude anywhere but most charts and globes of the earth show the first circle of latitude 60 nm from the equator, both north and south.

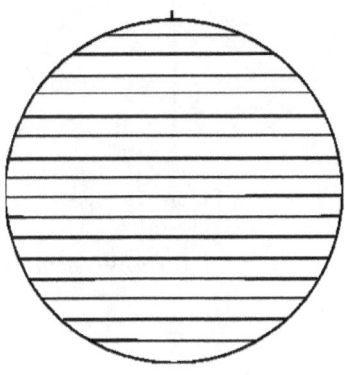

Figure 24

The globe in figure 24 shows parallels of latitude every ten degrees, (600 miles).

This first circle north of the equator is said to be 1' north latitude. Each nautical mile is equal to a minute of latitude, so 90 miles north of the equator is called $1°$, 30' north. My boat in the Houston area is $29°$, 30' north latitude which means 1770 miles north of the equator. (29.5 x 60 = 1770).

$90°$ north would be a little stake in the snow called the North Pole and is 5,400 miles from the equator.

Next, we need to understand longitude. The longitude lines are half circles around the globe and are not parallel to each other. See figure 25. To draw these circles, you start at one pole and draw a straight line the other pole. The beginning place for numbering these longitude lines is Greenwich, England which is $000°$ longitude.

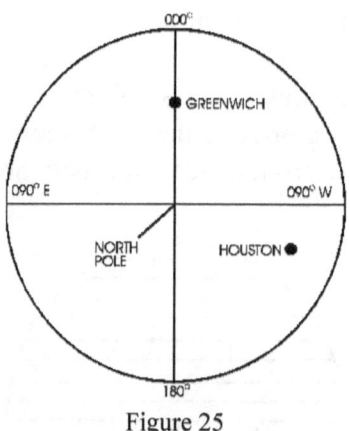

Figure 25

The globe in figure 25 shows a view looking down at the North Pole.

The longitude lines are numbered in a westerly direction from Greenwich, England. They are labeled

West, from 000° to 180°. The 180° line is referred to as the International Date Line. As you continue west from the 180° line, the numbers decrease to Greenwich and are labeled East.

Remember: Each minute of latitude, measured vertically, is one mile, but minutes of longitude, measured horizontally, are not equal to one mile (except at the equator), because longitude lines are not parallel.

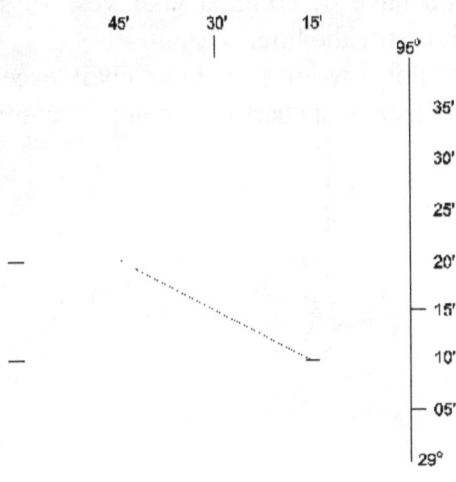

Figure 26

Use the parallel rules across the page for 29° 10' and 95° 15' making a light mark with a sharp pencil. The finer the point, the more accurate the reading. Do the same at 29° 20' North and 95° 45' West. After the two points are established, determine the distance with dividers, setting one point of the dividers on each point you have marked. Without changing the setting, move the dividers to the vertical scale on the side. Since each minute of latitude is equal to one mile, then twenty-five minutes would be 25 miles.

Figure 26 is an example for locating two geographic points on a chart and measuring the distance between them. The first point is located at 29° 10' North, and 95° 15' West. The second is located at 29° 20' North and 95° 45' West.

The example in figure 27 shows how to use parallel rules to find the true course from point "A" to point "B." After the course is determined, write it above the line, C 345°. If you have determined your vessel's speed, you will write it below the line.
Never plot anything on your chart except TRUE. There is no place on a chart for a compass course.

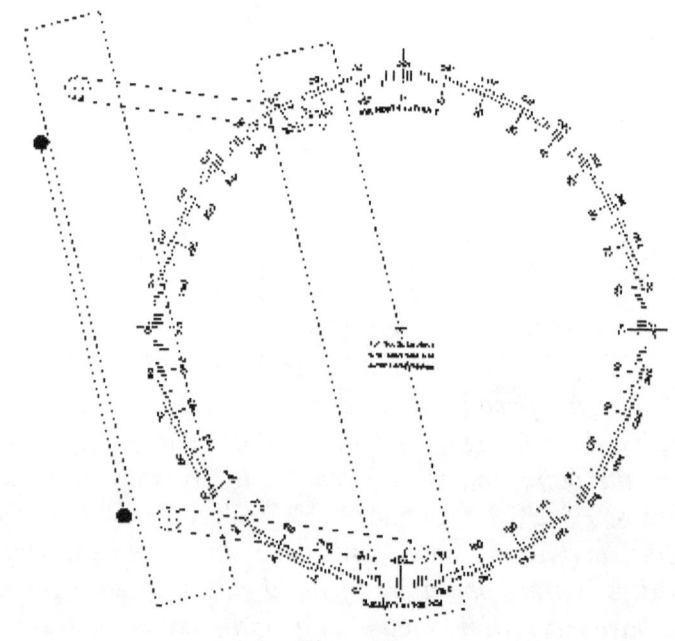

Figure 27

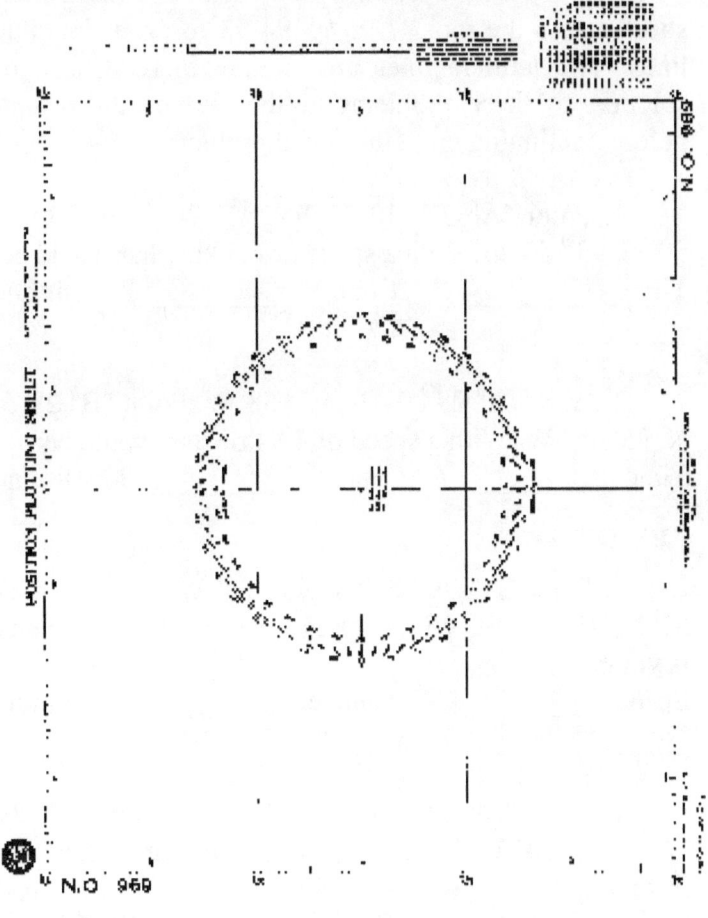

Figure 28

Figure 28 is a very small sample plotting sheet. You can purchase a full scale version (about 16" x 21") at various marine specialty and chart stores. You can have the original copied at any copy or architectural supply center. However, the copies may cost as much as purchasing the plotting sheets.

Captain Jack's Complete Navigation, By Jack I. Davis

Below are nine plotting problems. Label the plotting sheet across the top: 97 96 95 94 93 for your longitude lines. The latitude lines are already there. Check our solution to these problems at the end of this chapter before continuing on to the stated problems.

1. Point "A" 27° 10' N, 95° 15' W. Point "B" 27° 50' N, 95° 50' W. With a speed of 6.5 kn what would be:
Time _____? Course _____? Distance _____?

2. Point "A" 28° 03' N, 95° 58' W. Point "B" 28°57' N, 95° 03' W. With a speed of 4.8 kn what would be:
Time _____? Course _____? Distance _____?

3. Point "A" 29° 58' N, 95° 55' W. Point "B" 29° 31' N, 95° 11' W. With elapsed time of 8 hr 16 min what is your:
Speed _____? Course _____? Distance _____?

4. Point "A" 29° 55' N, 94° 17' W. Point "B" 29° 16' N, 94° 54' W. With elapsed time of 7 hr 13 min what is your:
Speed _____? Course _____? Distance _____?

5. Point "A" 29° 05' N, 94° 45' W. Point "B" 28° 46' N, 93° 56' W. With a speed of 8.3 kn what would be your:
Time _____? Course _____? Distance _____?

6. Point "A" 28° 28' N, 93° 48' W. Point "B" 29° 03' N, 94° 54' W. With a speed of 9.7 kn what would be your:
Time _____? Course _____? Distance _____?

7. Point "A" 29° 03' N, 94° 54' W. Point "B" 27° 55' N, 95° 09' W. With elapsed time of 9 hr 56 min what is your:
Speed _____? Course _____? Distance _____?

8. Point "A" 27° 55' N, 95° 06' W. Point "B" 27° 10' N, 93° 49' W. With elapsed time of 6 hr 42 min what is your:
Speed _____? Course _____? Distance _____?

9. Point "A" 27° 10' N, 93° 48' W. Point "B" 28° 05' N, 94° 08' W. With elapsed time of 8 hr 59 min what is your:
Speed _____? Course _____? Distance _____?

You will need one or more new plotting sheets to complete the remainder of the questions. Be certain to number the sheet according to the problem you are working.

10. You take three hours to run between marker "A" at 27° 18' N, 91° 50' W, and marker "B" at 27° 37' N, 91° 00' W. The inner compass rose on your chart is affected 011° W and your deviation card indicates a 006° E error. What is your true course _____, compass course _____, magnetic course _____, distance run _____, and speed _____?

11. Point Alpha is located at 29° 00' N and 91° 00' W and bears 275 PSC. Platform Bravo at 29° 10' N and 91° 00' W bears 325 PSC. The chart's inner compass rose indicates a variation of 15° west. The deviation from your deviation card at the time of the sightings was 10° east. There is a current setting SW at 2 knots. After your sighting of Alpha and Bravo, you run two hours on a true course of 045° and then drop anchor. Your speed through the water is 15 knots.

    a. Your position from the two sightings _____ ? (Fix)

    b. Your estimated position after the two hour run _____ ?

Label a course line with direction and speed. Above the course line place a capital C followed by three figures to indicate the course steered. The course label should indicate true direction. Below the course line and under the direction label, place a capital S followed by figures representing the speed in knots. Since the course is always given in degrees true and speed in knots, it is not necessary to indicate the units or the reference direction.

Definitions:
Estimated Position - Takes into consideration set and drift, and although it's not a fix it is a major improvement over a DR.
Speed of Advance - The same as speed over the bottom.
Set - The direction the current is going.
Drift - The speed of the current.
Distance Made Good - The geographical distance actually covered.
Speed Made Good - The speed over the bottom.

DR - Your dead reckoning position which takes into consideration only speed through the water and heading.

12. FIRST LEG. You leave your mooring and steer a course of 111° PSC to "C" platform, 17.5 miles distant at 29° 05' N and 89° 30' W. As you cast off, you note a current setting in a westerly direction. Your knot meter indicates 15 knots. Your underway time to "C" platform is 1 hour 16 minutes. Variation in this locality is 12° west. The deviation on this heading is 009° west.

    a. True course to "C" _____ ?

    b. Drift _____ ?

    c. Where was your mooring buoy _____ ?

SECOND LEG. You leave "C" and head for "D" a barge which is located at 29° 59' N and 89° 05' W. It takes five hours to complete this run.

    d. What is your true course _____ ?

    e. What is your compass course _____ ?
    f. What is the distance run _____ ?

    g. What is your speed _____ ?

You must assume the set and drift will remain the same.

13. FIRST LEG. At 1000 you leave your position at 28° 10' N and 89° 55' W steering a course of 081° PSC at 14.5 knots until 1130. Variation in this area is 19° east and deviation is 10° west.

a. What is your 1130 position _____?

b. What is your true course _____?

SECOND LEG. At 1130 you change course to 330° true and increase speed to 16 knots. The current is setting NW at 3 knots.

c. What is your 1530 DR position _____?

d. What is your 1530 EP _____?

e. What was your speed of advance from 1130 to 1530 _____?

f. What was your course made good from 1130 to 1530 _____?

THIRD LEG. At 1530 you change course to 222° true and reduce speed to 15 knots. The set and drift remain the same.

g. What is your 1700 DR position _____?

h. What is your 1700 EP _____?

14. FIRST LEG. You depart 28° 30' N, 89° 40' W on a course of 035° PSC at 0900 at a speed of 12 knots. Variation in your locality is 11° east. You calculate the deviation on that heading from your deviation table to be 16° west.

a. Your true course _____?

b. Your 1300 DR position _____?

SECOND LEG. At 1300. you alter course to 020° true and reduce speed to 10.5 knots. You encounter a current with a westerly set and drift of 4 knots.

    c. Your 1500 DR position _____?

    d. Your 1500 EP _____?

    e. The distance run from 1300 to 1500 _____?

    f. The course made good on this leg _____?

THIRD LEG. At 1500 you change course to 047° PSC and increase speed to 13.3 knots. There is no appreciable current.

    g. Your 1640 DR position _____?

    h. The total distance run from 0900 to 1640 _____?

    i. Your average speed from 0900 to 1640 _____?

15. At 2207 local time, Friday, January 15, you obtain a fix on lighthouse Martha at 27° 00' N, 89° 30' W bearing 132° PSC and drilling rig Kabar bearing 230° PSC. The drilling rigs position is 27° 00' N, 90° 10' W. Variation is 10° west. Your speed is 16 knots and your course is 090° true. The current is setting west at 3 knots. You run until Saturday, January 16 at 007 when you anchor.

    a. Your position at 2207 _____?

b. Your DR position at anchor _____?

　　c. Your EP at anchor _____?

　　d. Speed made good _____?

　16. FIRST LEG. You depart 1117, production platform "Amigo" at 28° 15' N, 89° 36' W, en route to derrick barge "Bravo" moored next to platform "Charlie" at 28° 36' N, 88° 56' W. You arrive on location at 1517. The variation is 007° W and your deviation is 006° W.

　　a. Distance run between Amigo and Charlie _____?

　　b. What compass course would you steer _____?

　　c. What was your speed from Amigo to Bravo _____?

　SECOND LEG. You depart the derrick barge at 1630 on a course of 103° PSC at a speed of 12 knots. At 1700 you sight rig Danny 30° off the port bow. At 1815 rig Danny bears 60° off the port bow.

　　d. The true bearing to rig Danny at 1700 _____? and at 1815 _____?

　　e. The PSC bearing of rig Danny at 1700 _____? and at 1815 _____?

　　f. The position of rig Danny from your two bearings _____?

g. The distance off Danny at the second bearing _____?

h. The distance off Danny when abeam _____?

Captain Jack's Complete Navigation, By Jack I. Davis

PLOTTING ANSWERS

SPEED	TIME	COURSE	DISTANCE
1. 6.5 kn	7 hr 55 min	$323°$	51.5 nm
2. 4.8 kn	14 hr 35 min	$041.5°$	70 nm
3. 5.75 kn	8 hr 16 min	$124°$	47.5 nm
4. 7.205 kn	7 hr 13 min	$220°$	52 nm
5. 8.3 kn	4 hr 34 min	$115.5°$	38 nm
6. 9.7 kn	7 hr 6.8 min	$302°$	68 nm
7. 6.84 kn	9 hr 56 min	$191°$	68 nm
8. 12.38 kn	6 hr 42 min	$123°$	83 nm
9. 6.456 kn	8 hr 59 min	$341°$	58 nm

10.   True course $066°$

       Compass Course $071°$

       Magnetic Course $077°$

Distance run 47 nm

Speed 15.66 kn

11.   a. 29° 00' N, 90° 50' W

     b. 29° 19' N. 90° 30' W

12.   a. 090°

     b. .93 kn

     c. 29° 05' N, 89° 30' W

     d. 035°

     e. 056°

     f. 68 nm

     g. 13.6 kn

13.   a. 28° 10' N, 89° 30' W

     b. 090°

     c. 29° 06' N, 90° 05' W

     d. 29° 17' N, 90° 11' W

     e. 19 kn

     f. 330°

     g. 29° 02' N, 90° 27' W

h. 29° 06' N, 90° 34' W

14. a. 030°

   b. 29° 11.8' N, 89° 13' W

   c. 29° 32' N, 89° 05' W

   d. 29° 32' N, 89° 13.7' W

   e. 19 nm

   f. 358°

   g. 29° 44' N, 89° 00' W

   h. 84 nm

   i. 10.95 kn

15. a. 27° 15' N, 89° 56' W

   b. 27° 15' N, 89° 20' W

   c. 27° 15.3' N, 89° 25' W

   d. 13 kn

16. a. 41.2 nm

   b. 071° PSC

   c. 10.25 kn

   d. 030°, 060°

e. 043°, 073°

f. 28° 49' N, 88° 22' W
g. 15 nm

h. 12.5 nm

Captain Jack's Complete Navigation, By Jack I. Davis

Chapter 11

FOLLOW YOUR NAVIGATIONAL PLAN

    Years before my sailing life got underway, I took a trip on a Morgan 41 Out Island with an experienced captain on an overnight sail from Miami to Bimini.

    I had never been on a sailboat and had never been out of sight of land. It was a stimulating experience, and in retrospect it was one of the key events that unchained me from a desk.

    Just before dawn the captain left me at the helm so he could get a little sleep. He told me the course to steer, left me with definite instructions not to change course and to call him if there was a problem of any kind.

    After a couple of hours, I spotted a sailboat on the horizon about thirty degrees off to starboard. I concluded he was probably approaching Bimini, probably had it in sight and we were, therefore, off course to the north. I changed course.

    The captain evidently sensed the change and came roaring out on deck immediately to give me the most severe chewing out I have had since I was a teenager.

"Don't ever change course unless you are instructed to change course."

This event made an indelible impression on me and even though over twenty years have gone by, I think of it often. Especially, when I have to leave a novice sailor at the helm.

I have found there is a strong tendency for sailors to quickly change their plan. This happens when they see something that suggests they are in the wrong place or going in the wrong direction.

Many times students have changed course "because the boat sails better" or "we go much faster on the other course." I have to remind them that sailing better or going faster in the wrong direction accomplishes very little towards their ultimate goal of arriving at a predetermined destination.

On one delivery, I was approaching the Fort Myers Beach outer marker, when one of my crew sang out that the marker was thirty degrees off to port. I was following the GPS heading which was adjusting for a strong current which was setting us north. Our vessel was not pointed at the marker even though we were making good the correct course to the marker.

Other crew joined in, certain we were going in the wrong direction. I ignored them just as I had the first crewman. By following the GPS course we got to within a hundred feet of the marker, at which time the GPS displayed this fact.

I had previously laid out a course of 328° to steer after we had the marker abeam. As soon as I turned on that course, my crew spotted a marker thirty degrees off to starboard and concluded, again, that we were going the wrong direction.

I am not saying these things as a put-down of my crew, but more so to emphasize the tendency of many sailors to forget the carefully laid out plan in favor of a haphazard judgment, which may be arrived at during the excitement of the moment.

To sum this up: Have a navigational plan. Be very careful about changing the plan without proper justification. Be very watchful of crew who may try to vary the plan.

Captain Jack's Complete Navigation, By Jack I. Davis

Chapter 12

FEAR, REMEMBRANCE, AND REALITY

Early in my sailing career, I was sailing my twenty-seven foot Erickson from Galveston to Padre Island (Port Isabel) with a couple of slightly more experienced sailors. Twenty-four hours into the trip or about four o'clock in the afternoon, the wind increased to forty knots and stayed. With the storm sails up I was going along well, but my experienced crew members were getting seasick.

I carried on until midnight, the wind not letting up, possibly increasing slightly and my crew was very sick. I didn't perceive any great danger to the boat, but I was becoming concerned about the crew.

Could people die from seasickness? I didn't know but I was getting worried.

I looked on the chart and found I wasn't far from the entrance to Matagorda Bay. I made a snap decision and changed course. Later, I began thinking about the wind direction and the way the cut into Matagorda Bay was laid out. It became clear the wind would be blowing straight down that cut.

What would the wave conditions be in the cut with this much wind? The charts didn't have that kind of information and I didn't know where else to look.

I knew there was a U. S. Coast Guard station on the bay, so I decided to call them on my VHF radio. I would ask them for any information about the storm I was in and see what they knew about the Matagorda cut.

By then I was less than fifteen miles away and they answered immediately. In response to my question about weather conditions, they read the last NOAA report. The same one I had been hearing for the last several hours. "Southeast winds 10 to 15 knots, seas 3 to 5 feet." When I told them I was experiencing light gale conditions, their reply was, "It must be a local disturbance because NOAA said 10 to 15." Of course my local disturbance had been going on for about six hours.

I asked about any possibly dangerous situations that might occur in the Matagorda cut with high winds blowing right down the middle. I said my charts didn't give me any insight into that problem.

Their response was: "You should have all the necessary charts aboard."

Well, so much for local knowledge assistance from the Coast Guard. I thought that if there was a grave and imminent danger, they surely would have told me. I still believe they could have handled this with better than stock answers.

I have been telling the *going-through-the-cut* story for many years: "When I got to the beginning of the channel between the jetties, the following seas changed from fifteen feet to thirty plus feet in a matter of minutes. There was practically no trough between the seas, I would be going down sharply, and then, Bang! I would be going back up. The pressure on the helm was tremendous. I had to brace myself and pull as hard as I could to keep from broaching."

The ups and downs, the pushing and pulling, went on for several hours. By the time I was inside and in smooth water I was absolutely exhausted.

A few years ago, I was back there on a boat delivery in good weather. The length of the cut through the jetties is less than one half mile. The time it would have taken me to get through, even in horrible weather, would have been ten minutes or so.

Looking back on this event, after tens of thousands of sailboat miles at sea and hundreds of real storms, I have had to rethink some of these stories. In the Matagorda cut that night the wind was probably less than forty knots, the seas less than thirty feet and the hours fighting these horrible conditions, were more like minutes.

My fear and exhaustion were real enough, but the rest was an exaggeration. Everything seemed so real, I didn't think I was exaggerating the hundreds of times I told the story.

In several cases where I have had inexperienced crew on boat deliveries, I have heard their stories told. Often the stories were so bizarre I could not believe I was on the same trip. These are good people who are not intentionally exaggerating, it's just the difference in perception of inexperience versus experience. To them the "horrible storm that lasted for hours" was in their minds "a horrible storm that lasted for hours." Whereas I recorded in my log, "We experienced a squall, with winds of thirty knots that lasted ten minutes."

With a green crew, as the wind increases they go through successions of growing fear. As the wind goes from a pleasant 15 knots to 30 knots the wind pressure doubles, the noise doubles and their fear doubles. At 40 knots we have storm sails up and everything has doubled again. At about 55 knots, everything has doubled again. We take down the storm sails and carry on under bare poles. Wind pressure, noise and fear have doubled again at 60 knots and without seeing it you can't believe it. If the wind continues to increase, this doubling effect continues about every 11 knots.

Then another strange thing happens. When the wind drops from 70 knots to 60 knots, it's twice as good as it was. From 60 knots to 50 knots everything is becoming downright pleasant. At 50 knots I have had the green crew come to ask if we can put up sails again. This is the same 50 knots, when the wind was building, where they were so scared they couldn't talk.

On one occasion I heard of a story being told by a former crew member about a knockdown we had experienced. I was on the same trip but somehow I missed the knockdown.

A knockdown occurs when the sailboat rolls over with the mast in the water, if not pointing straight down. In my career this has only happened once and it was a freak situation, having to do more with the boat configuration rather than the storm.

The knockdown the crew was talking about was in a situation where we were laying ahull in a storm for twenty-seven hours, and the boat fell on its side three or four times. The mast never got close to going under and the danger to boat and crew was minimal, although the ride was unpleasant.

The crew member really believed he had been in a knockdown. I logged, "Rough seas and an unpleasant ride which interfered with my coffee drinking and gin rummy."

The Matagorda cut situation, even though I misjudged it, can be a very real danger. The problem arises when the water is running out of the bay through the cut and the wind is blowing the opposite direction.

Captain Jack's Complete Navigation, By Jack I. Davis

This causes the seas to, not only get larger than usual, but also closer together. Through the years I have witnessed this problem at the Galveston Bay inlet, the Penscola Bay inlet, the Gulf Stream around the straits of Florida and up the east coast. When the wind is blowing against the Gulf Stream, the seas become very dangerous. I have described them many times as square waves. My conclusion is to avoid these situations anyway you can because they can do some real damage.

But then you say, "What if I can't avoid it. What if I have to go?" These have been the last words spoken by many sailors and aviators.

You never have to go!!!!! There are always alternatives. The first thing to do is a little book work ahead of time. The *US Coast Pilot* (which I did not have aboard that stormy night) has worlds of information about almost any navigable entrance. In the case of the Matagorda Ship Channel, the *Pilot* shows tidal currents of up to three knots. Another book, *Tidal Current Tables* gives the times of these tidal changes.

By knowing the outgoing tide could be running three knots and the time of its peak run was the time I happened on the scene, I could have hoved-to off shore for two or three hours and had a smooth run into the bay.

If I could have known how steep the waves were going to be and how hard it would be to control the helm, I would have preferred a few hours of laying ahull.

The Gulf stream is a different problem as it runs up to four knots all the time. The secret is not to be there if heavy winds are blowing against it, which sometimes cannot be predicted.

The saving grace is that almost anywhere along the straits of Florida and up the east coast, you are not far from sanctuary. Many times I have aborted trips across the stream and pulled into a safe anchorage for a few hours to avoid a severe beating.

Now that I've scared everyone with horror stories let me summarize:

1. The wind will not and cannot blow your boat over, it just cannot happen. On a monohull sailing vessel the wind can only push the boat over on its side so far, then there is nothing left for the wind to blow against. The boat will right itself and the process will begin again.

2. Under usual conditions (if there is such a thing), there is a strict consistency in wave height and the distance between wave tops. The more wind velocity, the higher the waves and the further apart they become. In a major storm in the Atlantic, which blew from one direction (north) for several days, the wave heights built to more than fifty feet. However, the distance between the tops was over one-quarter of a mile. I carried on under storm sails through the whole thing and the sailing was not unpleasant.

3. The danger comes when there is tidal movement one way and the wind the opposite. I have had to hove-to in 35 knots of wind in these conditions when the seas were only fifteen feet but they weren't fifty feet apart, and as I said before, square.

4. If you study the weather broadcast and pick your weather accordingly, you should not have to undergo major trauma on the water. Learning as much as you can about the handling and repair of your boat, along with the proper charts, books, navigational tools, safety gear and back-up gear will give you piece of mind knowing you can handle any situation.

SAILING TERMS SPOKEN EVERY DAY

BITTER END - The last link in a ship's anchor rode and usually attached to the ship by bolt or snap. If you let out all of a ship's anchor rode, you come to the bitter end. The trailing or loose end of a line.

BLAZER - Jacket which derives its name from HMS (Her Majesty's Ship) BLAZER whose captain, in 1845, dressed his crew in special blue and white striped jerseys.

CABOOSE - Housing for the chimney of the cook's galley on a merchant vessel.

CUT AND RUN - To cut through a hemp anchor rode so that the ship can get underway in an emergency. (Or release the bolt from the bitter end.)

DOLDRUMS - Area of low pressure near the equator between the trade winds.

FENDER - Device used to prevent damage by impact, or by chaffing or rubbing.

HIGH AND DRY - Condition of a ship aground so that the tide, falling away, brings her keel above water.

LAID-UP - Said of a vessel when she has been un-rigged and her gear dismantled.

LAND SHARK - Lawyer. Considered to be unlucky to have aboard for any purpose.

LANDMARK - Any distinctive feature ashore, such as a lighthouse, beacon or unusual contour of land, that can serve as an aid to navigation.

LEEWAY - Sideways drift of a vessel to leeward of her course. It was imperative to plot a course that would allow enough leeway to clear a potentially dangerous area.

ON AN EVEN KEEL - Said of a vessel when her keel is horizontal and she draws the same draught of water both forward and aft.

PIPE DOWN - Proper order on early sailing ships to be quiet.

QUEEN OF THE ROAD - A vessel close-hauled and having the right of way.

SCUTTLEBUTT - Lidded cask in which fresh water was kept for daily use. (And where you picked up the latest gossip.)

SON OF A GUN - Derived from the period of time when wives of seamen lived aboard in harbor, (sometimes at sea) and had to give birth between the guns, since the deck gear had to be kept clear.

TAKE A DIFFERENT TACK - A vessel beating to weather changes course from to side to side, is said to be tacking.

TAKEN ABACK - Surprised - Stopped short, as when the wind suddenly changed and back winded your sails, bringing your vessel to a sudden halt.

TOUCH AND GO - To run a vessel aground but float her almost immediately.

UNDERWAY - Not tied to a mooring or to shore.

PART TWO

CELESTIAL

NAVIGATION

Captain Jack's Complete Navigation, By Jack I. Davis

INTRODUCTION

With the incredible advances in electronic navigation equipment, especially the development of the satellite system, small boat navigation is so simple I'm surprised anyone would make the effort to learn basic navigation.

The greater effort of learning celestial navigation, I thought, would be an effort that would go the way of the dinosaurs. To my surprise basic navigation is in good demand and I have more requests for classes in celestial than ever before.

There remains a fear the electronics may fail. To a greater extent my students want the security that comes with knowledge and in the case of celestial, they want the bragging rights. Very few sailors ever get far enough along with the study of celestial navigation for it to be useful to them. Most sailors at a yacht club bar will begin to fade away when a few sailors start talking about reducing sights, cocked hat star sights, etc.

Before the electronics age, most long-range sailors who claimed to know celestial navigation, only understood the "noon sight." As you will learn the noon sight is a very small part that can be learned by almost anyone in a matter of minutes.

When I decided to go cruising, I knew I had to learn celestial because the only electronic aid available at the time was the old Loran A, a huge, expensive instrument which I knew I couldn't afford on my limited budget.

Captain Jack's Complete Navigation, By Jack I. Davis

I read that people would sit on the end of a dock and learn celestial from a boat neighbor, but I didn't know anyone who knew celestial. In one sailing magazine story a new sailor picked up a book on celestial navigation and after a few hours reading was qualified to go around the world using his sextant. If it's that easy why don't I just dig in and learn? I tried not one, but several books on the subject and after many days of reading had not learned anything. During the fifth book the light finally penetrated my thick skull and I started to enjoy the learning experience. Many more days went by before I could honestly say, "I understand."

After arriving at this understanding, I spent several months getting the boat ready to go. Shortly before it was "cast off" time, I realized I couldn't remember enough celestial navigation to work a sight. To my chagrin it was almost as hard to relearn celestial navigation as it was to learn it in the first place.

Finally, all came together and I began my cruising life, with my celestial navigation working very well. This sort of life came down to a few days of sailing and weeks of hanging on the hook, gunkholing and exploring, amounting to nothing more than coast piloting. When it was time for the second leg of my cruise, I had forgotten celestial again.

All in all, I probably relearned celestial navigation six times, with each time being virtually as difficult as the first time. It wasn't until I agreed to teach celestial navigation to a group of my sailing buddies that I got the material organized well, thereby getting it straight in my mind. Using this organization as a technique in the class room I find my students are better able to remember what they learn. Part of this technique involves NOT using preprinted forms. With forms, the student is learning how to fill out forms and retains very little of the purpose behind the procedure. If the navigator addicted to forms runs out of forms or -- God forbid -- they get blown overboard or soaked with sea water, then he is no longer able to find his way. That would be no different than having a GPS with dead batteries.

Please understand my methods are not necessarily scientific perfection. They are more of a method for you to find your way with a sextant, reducing the sights on the back of a matchbook while leaning against the mast, if it is ever necessary to do so.

Jack I. Davis

These examples, along with their answers, are derived from the 1999 Nautical Almanac. If a 1999 Nautical Almanac is not available to you, all problems can be calculated but you will arrive at slightly different answers.

The purpose of the exercises is to teach you the fundamentals of working navigation problems with an almanac. Whatever version of the Nautical Almanac you use, these fundamentals remain the same.

CHAPTER 13
THE SEXTANT

The sextant measures the height above the horizon of a celestial object, (sun, moon, planet or star), in degrees, minutes and fractions of a minute. Some sextants show seconds instead of a fraction of a minute.

What good is this to us? How does this help us find our position? To demonstrate, let's look at Polaris, the North Star.

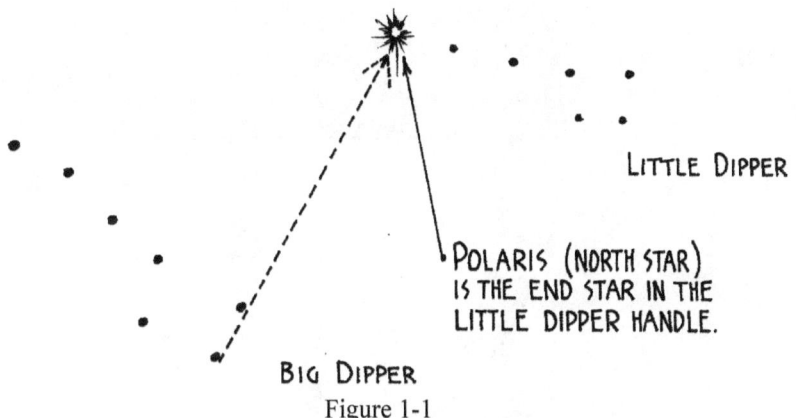

Figure 1-1

Our latitude in southeast Texas is about 30 degrees North. When we use our sextant to shoot a sight of Polaris we face north and find the star is about 30 degrees above the horizon. If we were in Nebraska, our latitude would be about 45 degrees North and facing north our sextant would show Polaris to be 45 degrees above the horizon. In fact if we move all the way north to the North Pole we would be at 90 degrees North latitude and our sextant would read 90 degrees height for Polaris, regardless of which direction we faced. Therefore, we can determine our latitude by measuring the altitude of Polaris.

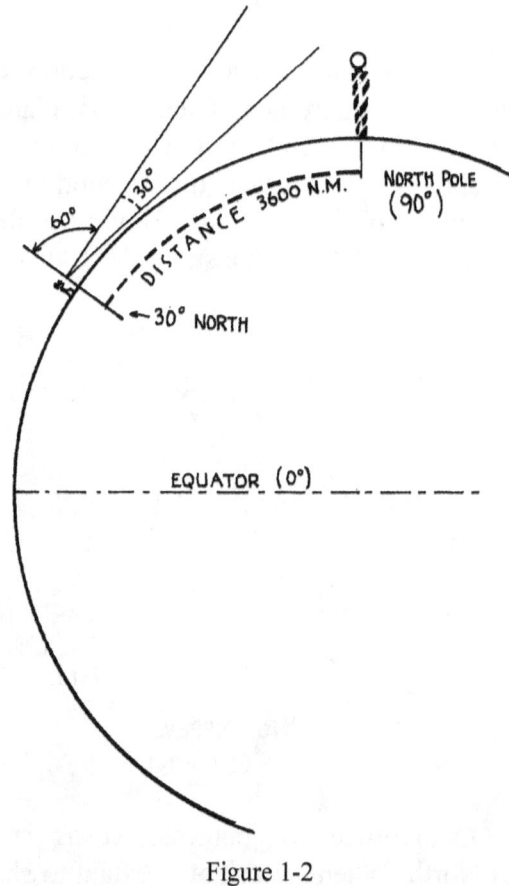

Figure 1-2

We can determine the distance we are away from the North Pole by measuring the height of Polaris. The point directly below a celestial object is called the GP (Ground Point). The GP of Polaris "wobbles" around the North Pole every twenty-four hours, so a sextant reading at dusk will be slightly off, as will a morning reading. An average of the two readings will be exact since the morning error and the evening error offset. The nautical almanac gives corrections for both.

POLARIS
How to find it
EQUATOR TO POLE

If a sextant reading is 30 degrees, subtract that from 90 degrees, which gives the co-altitude of Polaris. In this example, that would be 60 degrees. Since each degree is equal to 60 nautical miles distance, 60 degrees times 60 miles equals 3600 miles, the distance from the North Pole.

Co-altitude x 60 miles = distance away. See figure 1-2.

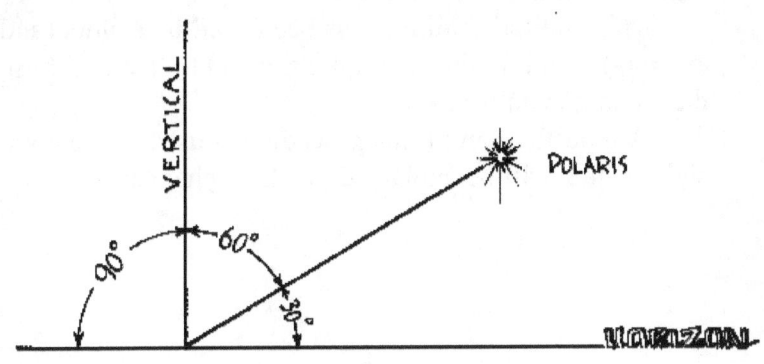

Figure 1-3

The early ocean navigators understood that you could find your latitude using the North Star.

They didn't have the very accurate sextants we have today. They had a crude instrument called an astrolabe, which would give them a rough reading. When Columbus discovered the entrance to San Juan Harbor, Puerto Rico, he knew (from the astrolabe) the entrance was at about 19 degrees North latitude. He didn't have a clue what his longitude was and for his purposes it didn't matter.

When he sailed back toward his home port, he sailed north until he arrived at the latitude of the Mediterranean entrance. There, he turned east and ran that latitude line until the Rock of Gibraltar came into view.

On his return trip to San Juan, he sailed from the Mediterranean, past the Rock of Gibraltar and sailed south to 19 degrees North. He followed that latitude line until Puerto Rico came into view.

The thousands of sailors who followed in Columbus's wake, said when traveling from the Mediterranean to the West Indies, you sail south until the butter melts, then turn right.

This "latitude sailing" has been used by sailors (and aviators) well into the electronic age and in fact I still use the technique on occasion.

A modification of this procedure is used in the noon sight, which will be explained in a later chapter.

Captain Jack's Complete Navigation, By Jack I. Davis

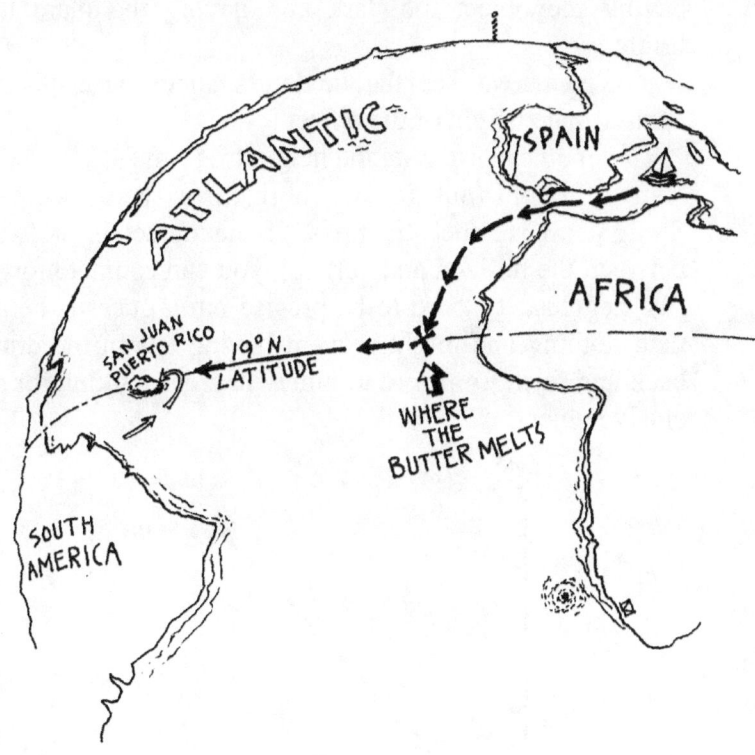

Figure 1-4

THE MED TO SAN JUAN

What do we see when we use our sextant to measure the altitude of an object?

First, face the object. This sounds simple, but it's a critical lesson to learn in finding the object in the sextant's telescope. One clue (with the sun) is to observe shadows that might help you find the precise direction.

You will want to use the mirror glass shades to cut the glare. You will have to experiment between having the object too dark and having the glare too bright.

Next we set the sextant's index arm to the approximate height of the object.

You can estimate the height this way:

Straight out to the horizon is zero degrees. Straight up is ninety degrees. If the object is halfway between the horizon and vertical, you can estimate forty-five degrees. It's hard to be precise but a guess is better than nothing and might prevent having to run the drum back and forth from zero to ninety degrees looking for an elusive object.

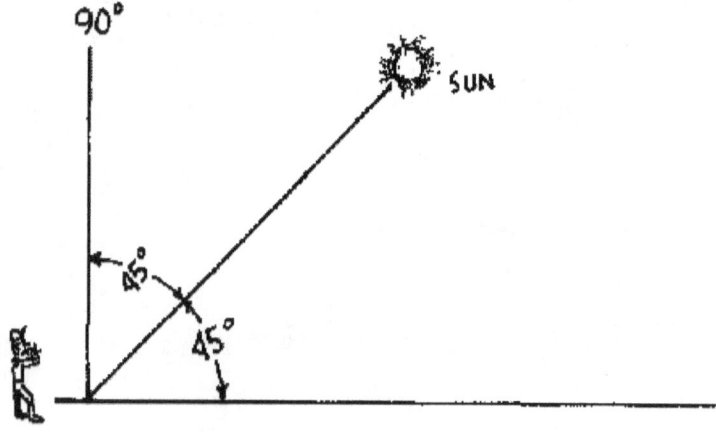

Figure 1-5

After you find the object, bring it down, slowly with the index arm and then fine tune it with the drum until it just touches the horizon. A sharp well-defined horizon is very important and you can improve the accuracy of your sights by adjusting the focus on your sextant's telescope.

If you're shooting stars or planets there will just be a dot on the horizon with no particular diameter to contend with, but with the sun or moon you have a choice; bringing the object down to where the bottom of the circle is just barely touching the horizon, which is called a "LOWER LIMB" sight or bringing the object down below the horizon to where the top of the circle is just barely touching the horizon, which is called an "UPPER LIMB" sight.

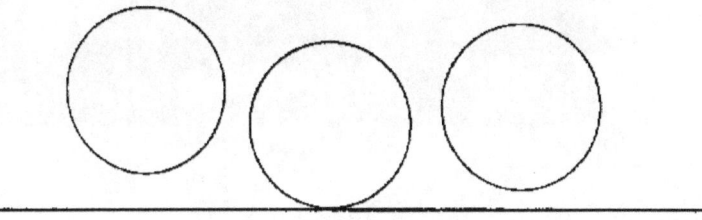

Figure 1-6

Rock the sextant back and forth to better determine the bottom of the arc.

There are, of course, other types of sextants but the two shown will cover most of the bases.

Next we look at close ups of two sextants.

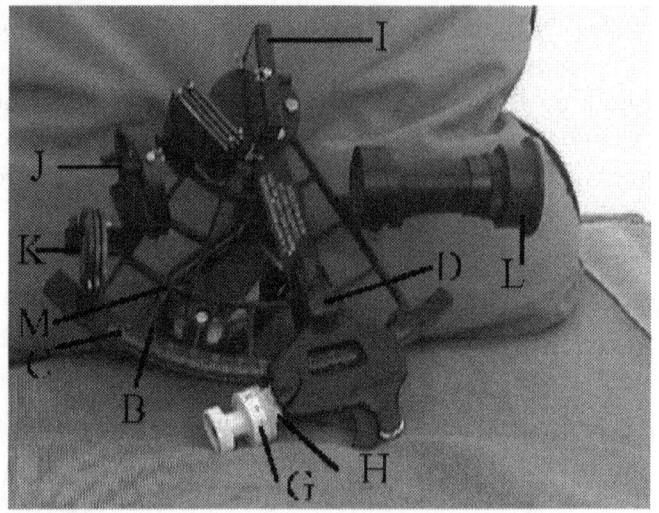

Figure 1-7

US Navy Mark 3 (Front)

MICROMETER DRUM SEXTANT

B. Limb
C. The arc (with teeth for each degree of arc)
D. Index arm (movable bar)
G. Micrometer drum (one complete turn moves the index arm one degree)
H. Vernier (aids in reading graduations of a degree)
I. Index mirror.
J. Horizon glass (half silvered next to frame)
K. Shade glasses.
L. Telescope.
M. Handle (holds batteries and switch for light)

Captain Jack's Complete Navigation, By Jack I. Davis

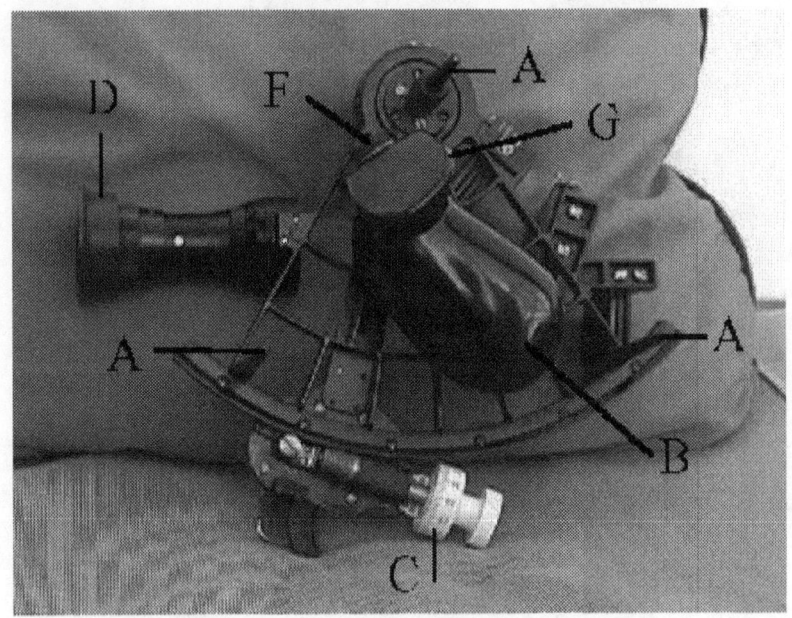

Figure 1-8

US Navy Mark 3 (Back)

A. Legs (3)
B. Handle
C. Micrometer drum
D. Rubber eye guard
F. Battery Cap
G. Light Switch

Captain Jack's Complete Navigation, By Jack I. Davis

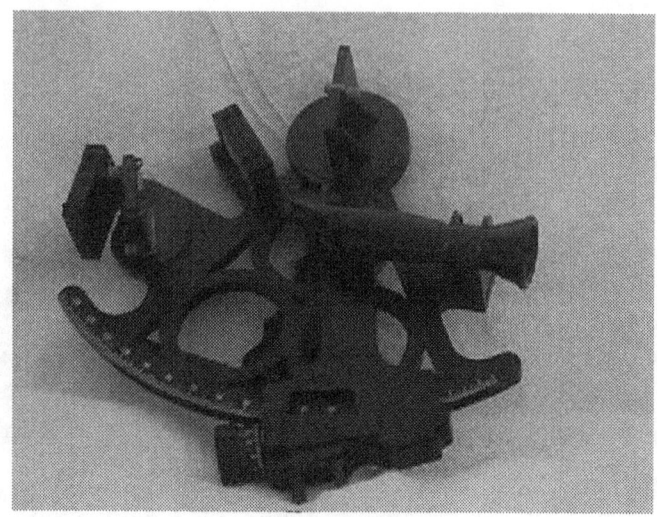

Figure 1-9

Davis Instrument Corp. (Front)

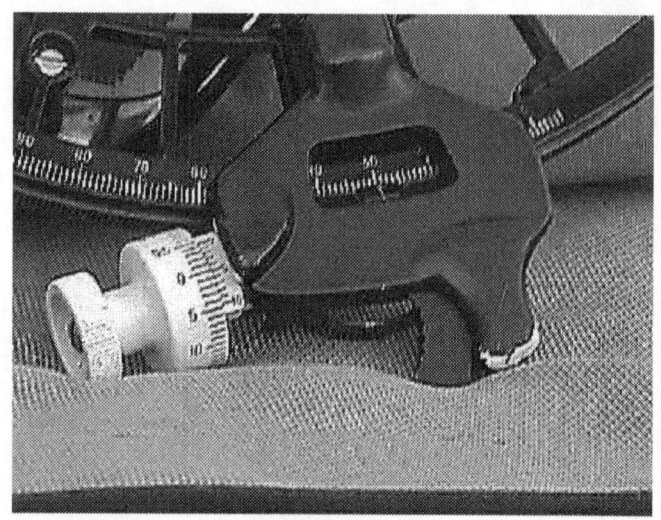

Figure 1-10

Mark 3 showing a reading of 29 55.5

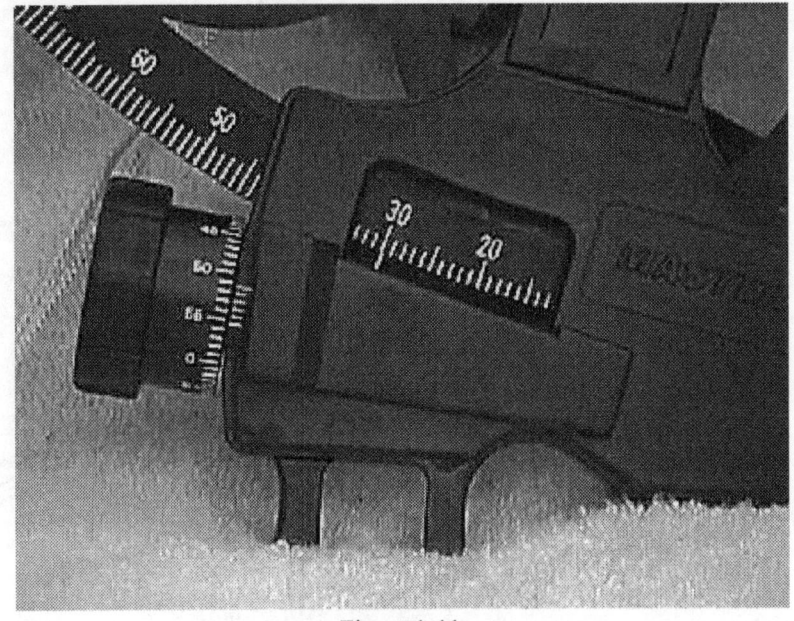

Figure 1-11

Davis - showing a reading of 29 51.4

A metal sextant similar to the Mark 3 is factory set and comes with an index error card that shows small errors existing in the sextant. Since these errors are tiny and insignificant, I ignore them. A deck officer on the QE2 might take them into consideration, but on a small boat they just get lost in the shuffle. If you want to check and adjust errors, use the procedure described below for plastic sextants.

On plastic sextants the index error can change easily, due to temperature variations and vibration. Therefore, index error should be checked on a regular basis. The manufacturer recommends checking it before each use.

On a correctly adjusted sextant, the two mirrors are always perpendicular to the frame, and become parallel to each other when the body and drum scales read zero.

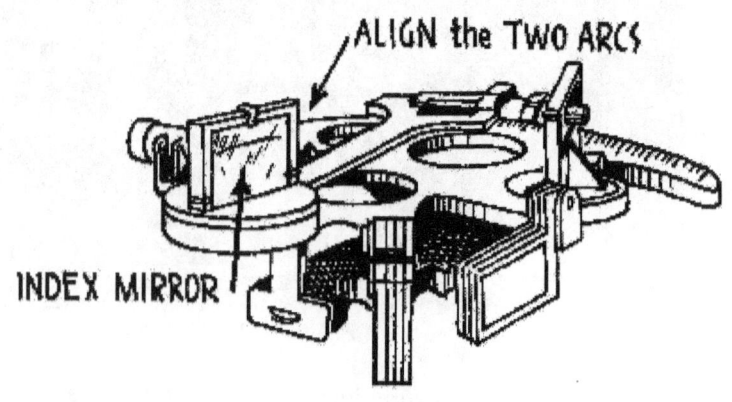

Figure 1-12

Index mirror is not perpendicular to the frame - reflected arc does not appear as continuous curve with the actual frame arc.

INDEX MIRROR ADJUSTMENT

Adjust the index mirror (the large movable mirror at the pivot of the index arm) so it is perpendicular to the frame. Set the instrument to approximately 50 degrees, holding the sextant horizontal, about eight inches from the eye, in the mirror until the frame arc is reflected. Move the instrument until you can see past the index mirror, frame arc and reflected arc. The two arcs should appear as one continuous curve. If they do not, turn the adjustment screw at the back of the index mirror until the two arcs come into alignment. See Figure 1-12.

Figure 1-13

(Left) Mirror horizon is not aligned with real horizon - index arm is not in proper position.

(Right) Mirror horizon and real horizon form a single straight line - index is properly positioned.

HORIZON MIRROR ADJUSTMENT

Adjust the horizon mirror (the small half-silvered mirror) for side error by making it perpendicular to the frame. Holding the sextant in your right hand, raise the instrument to your eye. Look at any horizontal straight edge, for example, the sea horizon or the roof of a building. Move the index arm back and forth. The real horizon will remain still, while the mirror horizon will appear only when the body and drum scales read close to zero. Line up the mirror horizon and the real horizon so both appear as a single straight line. See Figure 1-13.

Figure 1-14

(Left) Horizon mirror screw too tight
(Center) Horizon mirror screw correctly adjusted
(Right) Horizon mirror screw too loose

Without changing the setting, look through the sextant at any vertical line, for example a flag pole or the vertical edge of a building. Swing the instrument back and forth across the vertical line. If the horizon mirror is not perpendicular to the frame, the line will seem to jump to one side as the mirror passes it. To correct this, slowly tighten or loosen the screw closest to the frame at the back of the horizon mirror until the vertical line no longer appears to jump. See Figure 1-14.

INDEX ERROR ADJUSTMENT

To remove the index error, set the sextant to 0 00 0 and look at the horizon. With the sextant still held to your eye, turn the screw farthest from the frame at the back of the horizon mirror until the two horizons move together and form one straight line. The two mirrors are now parallel to each other. See Figure 1-15.

Figure 1-15

(Left) Horizon mirror and index mirror not parallel
(Right) Horizon mirror and index mirror parallel

To be certain the sextant is correctly adjusted, it should still be set at 0 00. The real and mirror horizons should remain in a single line when the instrument is rocked or inclined from side to side. See Figure 1-16.

Figure 1-16

On a correctly adjusted sextant, the real and mirror horizons remain in a single line when the instrument is rocked from side to side.

You should know how to adjust your sextant for index error but it is not necessary to remove it entirely. Note the error and correct the reading each time the sextant is used. As much as 6' index error is allowable. To find index error, hold the sextant in your right hand and look at the sea horizon. Move the index arm and the micrometer drum until the real and mirror horizons appear as a single straight line. If the sextant reads 0 00, there is no index error. If the sextant reads anything but zero, the difference must be added or subtracted from each subsequent sight.

CHAPTER 14

THE NAUTICAL ALMANAC

The nautical almanac is an intensely interesting book of valuable information for the celestial navigator.

All almanac references in this book are based on the 1999 Nautical Almanac.

A2 ALTITUDE CORRECTION TABLES 10 TO 90 SUN, STARS, PLANETS

The yellow pages in the commercial edition will be used to refine your sextant sight. When shooting your sight the number you find is called the sextant altitude of the object. When working the sight, label this number "Hs". Big H, little s.

Get in the habit of learning, remembering and using these symbols correctly, as it will help you retain the overall concept of what we are doing.

At the top of the yellow page, the far left column reads: OCT. - MAR. SUN APR. - SEPT.

This is the table we use for corrections to sun sights. These corrections will be labeled MAIN corrections, and deal with the diameter of the sun and refraction.

Refraction is the bending effect you see when you stick a straight pole into clear water. The pole appears to bend and the end of the pole is not where it seems to be. The rays of the sun unbend when they come through our atmosphere and, like the bending pole, it is not where it appears.

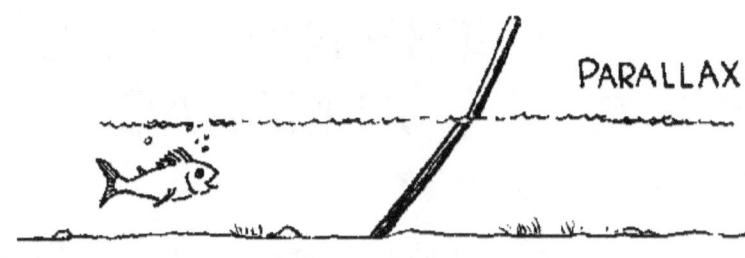

Figure 2-1

The middle column reads: STARS AND PLANETS

This table is for corrections to star and planet sights. There is little diameter to consider with these bodies, so corrections are only for refraction.

The last column on the far right reads: DIP

This table is used to determine the height of eye, which is how high our sextant is above sea level at the time of the sight.

Figure 2-2

We begin with DIP. At the top of this table you will see two columns, both labeled "Ht. of Eye Correction". The column on the left gives you a choice of height in meters or feet, with the appropriate correction in between.

The column on the left has several different choices not included in the first column.

Meters
1.0 - 1.'8
1.5 - 2.'2
2.0 - 2.'5
etc.

The next section covers meters 20 through 48.
The next section covers feet 2 - 4 - 6 - 8 - 10.
The final section covers feet 70 through 155 in 5 foot increments.

The sextant sight of the sun is 29^0 21.'7, which is 29 degrees, 21 minutes and .7 (7/10) of a minute.

In the DIP column the correction for height of eye at 8 feet is -2.'7 which is 2 minutes and .7 (7/10) of a minute. Please notice that I show minus 2.'7. All dip corrections are minus unless you are shooting below sea level, which is very unlikely. We write this on a piece of paper:

Hs	29^0 21.'7
DIP	-2.'7
Ha	29^0 19.'0

This is the apparent altitude correction for height of eye.

Using the far left column, select the appropriate period of time: October through March, or April through September. Use October - March for this calculation.

Using the apparent altitude (Ha) of 29^0 19.'0, look down that column to find the MAIN correction. You'll find the Ha number falls between 29^0 15' and 30^0 46'.

At this point you have two choices: Lower limb and upper limb. Usually when shooting the sun, you will shoot lower limb sights. The exception would be when a cloud covers the lower edge of the sun but you can clearly see the top. You could shoot the upper limb or wait until the cloud moves and shoot the lower limb.

Between 29^0 15' and 30^0 46' the correction is +14.'6 (or -17.'7 for the upper limb).

Continue on with our notes:

```
Hs      29⁰ 21.'7
DIP         -2.'7
Ha      29⁰ 19.'0
MAIN   + 14.'6   (I have labeled this MAIN)
Ho      29⁰ 33.'6
```

This is labeled "Ho" and is the final product of our sun sight which is the HEIGHT OBSERVED.

The DIP is a small correction, but the MAIN correction is fairly large, because it is dealing with the diameter of the sun and refraction. If we could bring the middle of the sun down to the horizon we would get rid of a lot of this correction. However, the middle is not marked on the sun!

When we have determined Ho, we have half the formula needed to plot our sight.

Next let's assume a star sight, sextant reading of:

```
Hs      32⁰ 15.'6
8' Dip      -2.'7
Ha      32⁰ 12.'9
```

Using this Ha refer to the left side of the STAR & PLANETS column, where we find our number falls between 32^0 00.'0 and 33^0 45.'0 which is -1.'5

<u>MAIN   -1.'5</u>
Ho 32^0 11.'4 (Our corrected star sight)

Planet sights are completed the same as star sights, with the exception of Venus and Mars which may require a small additional correction depending on the time of year and the altitude. These corrections are noted at the right side of the STAR & PLANETS column.

The following are exercises to check your proficiency in correcting sextant sights. For each sight I show the date, local time of the sight (military time), type of object and your height of eye. For a sun sight I designate LL or UL for Lower Limb or Upper Limb. The answers are at the end of the chapter.

For the accuracy, you need to line your numbers up very neatly, and remember you can't have an answer with more than 59.'9 minutes.

(1) Sun LL   (2) Sun LL   (3) Dubhe   (4) Jupiter
    4-11-99   7-15-99   1-03-99   10-19-99
    1115 32   1521 56   1753 23   0613 54
    Hs 42^0 08.'8   Hs 36^0 59.'3   Hs 21^0 03.'6   Hs 33^0 44.'6
    8' Dip   6' Dip   10' Dip   8' Dip

(5) Mars   (6) sun UL   (7) Rigil   (8) Canopus
9-15-99   6-01-99   2-28-99   12-03-99
1842 45   1015 55   0600 53   0712 32

Hs $51°16.'8$ Hs $36°16.'3$ Hs $44°34.'2$ Hs $41°01.'3$
10' Dip   6' Dip   10' Dip   10' Dip

There are several ways to record your time. With two people, one can hold the sextant and the other the time piece. When the shooter has it exactly the way he wants it he says, "Mark," and the timer records the time.

If alone use a stop watch. Holding the sextant with the right hand and the stop watch with the left, get the object just right. At the point you would say "mark", start the stop watch. Pick a period of exact elapsed time on the watch (five minutes will work well) and stop the stop watch. Whatever it shows at that point is subtracted from the five minutes giving you the exact time of the sight.

If GP (Ground Point) of the object you are shooting is traveling at a speed of nine hundred knots, an error of a few seconds time can throw your plotting miles off course.

ANSWERS

(1) Sun LL	(2) Sun LL	(3) Star-Dubhe
4-11-99	7-15-99	1-03-99
1115 32	1521 56	1753 23
Hs 42^0 08.'8	Hs 36^0 59.'3	Hs 21^0 03.'6
8' Dip - 2.'7	6' Dip - 2.'4	10' Dip - 3.'1
Ha 42^0 06.'1	Ha 36^0 56.'9	Ha 21^0 00.'5
LL MAIN +14.'9	LL MAIN +14.'7	MAIN - 2.'5
Ho 42^0 21.'0	Ho 37^0 11.'6	Ho 20^0 58.'0

(4) Planet-Jupiter	(5) Planet-Mars	(6) Sun UL
10-19-99	9-15-99	6-01-99
0613 54	1842 45	1015 55
Hs 33^0 44.'6	Hs 51^0 16.'8	Hs 36^0 16.'3
8' Dip - 2.'7	Dip - 3.'1	Dip - 2.'4
Ha 33^0 41.'9	Ha 51^0 13.'7	Ha 36^0 13.'9
MAIN -1.'5	MAIN -0.'8	MAIN -17.'1
Add +0.'1		
Ho 33^0 40.'5	Ho 51^0 12.'9	Ho 35^0 56.'8

(7) Star-Rigil	(8) Star-Canopus
2-28-99	12-03-99
0600 53	0712 32
Hs $44°$ 34.'2	Hs^0 41 01.'3
10' Dip - 3.'1	10' Dip - 3.'1
Ha $44°$ 31.'1	Ha $40°$ 58.'2
MAIN - 1.'0	MAIN - 1.'1
Ho $44°$ 30.'1	Ho $40°$ 57.'1

CHAPTER 15

GP - THE DAILY PAGES

GP stands for Ground Point or in some books, Geographical Position. It doesn't make a difference which one you remember, but you should understand the concept.

Every visible, celestial object is directly overhead some where on earth. Regardless of where you are, it's high noon somewhere. The spot directly under the sun is the GP of the sun at that instant.

That GP spot moves, from east to west, across the face of the earth, at 900 knots. Divided, it's 15 nautical miles per minute or .25 nautical miles every second. When you start shooting sights, you have to continually turn the sextant drum to keep up with the movement. The nautical almanac gives us the GP of the sun, moon, brightest planets and a number of the brighter stars for every second of every day.

In order to accomplish this monumental task some procedures and short cuts have been adopted. A guided tour of the almanac will help you understand how this works.

Turn to June 21. Look at the page on the right which gives us the GP of the sun for June 21, 22 and 23, which are Monday, Tuesday and Wednesday.

The heading of the first column on the left reads UT, which stands for Universal Time. This is the new designation for GMT, Greenwich Mean Time.

This time is broadcast on several short wave radio channels from WWV Fort Collins, Colorado. They are 2.5, 5, 10, 15, 20 and 25 MHz. Listening to those channels, you will hear a little tick every second. Once per minute a voice announces the hour and minute, saying Universal Coordinated Time. Five minutes after the hour, for five minutes, the voice gives storm information for the Atlantic and Gulf.

Another station in Hawaii designated WWVH gives the same information on the same frequencies as WWV, with the exclusion of 25 MHz. This station includes storm warning information for the Pacific. Canada also maintains a UT broadcast station.

How do we determine local time from UT and how do we find UT when we have shot our sight at local time?

Greenwich England is in the dead center of the first of twenty-four time zones (12 West of Greenwich and 12 East of Greenwich). Each time zone is fifteen degrees wide. Each degree is made up of sixty minutes and each minute equals one mile at the equator. Therefore, each degree equals sixty miles. 60 times 15 degrees equals 900 miles, the distance across each time zone. The sun goes through one time zone per hour. Since the GP of the sun is traveling at 900 knots, the circumference of the earth is 900 times 24 or 21,600 nautical miles.

On the far right side of a sheet of paper, make a small box, about 1/2 inch square. Put a zero in the box to indicate Greenwich. Make a second box, attached to the left side of the first and put a 15 in that box. Continue making boxes for 30, 45, 60, 75, 90, 105, 120, 135, 150, 165 and 180.

Go back and label each box starting with 15 as 1, the first time zone. 30 is 2, 45 is 3, 60 is 4, 75 is 5, 90 is 6, 105 is 7, etc.

The center of the 180 box is the International Date Line -- time zone 12. If you want to continue on, start another line and put 165 in the first box -- time zone 11 (East of Greenwich). 150 is next and is zone 10 and so on until you are back at Greenwich -- time zone 0.

When daylight savings goes into effect, the first Sunday in April, (daylight savings ends the last Sunday in October), local time moves forward one hour.

Now, back to the Nautical Almanac and the UT column. Assume we have shot a sight of the sun at 1015 23 local time on the 21st day of February. Daylight savings is not in effect so we must add 6 hours giving us 1615 23 which is the time at Greenwich when we shot our sight.

One column to the right is GHA and Dec at the top of the column. These stand for Greenwich Hour Angle which is equivalent to Longitude and Declination, which is equivalent to Latitude. We will discuss hour angles more later.

Go down the UT column to 1600, move over one column and record the numbers 56^0 35.'5 under the GHA column and S 10^0 33.4 under the Dec column (note the 10 is not repeated every hour, so you have to assume it's there). This is the geographical position (GP) of the sun at 1600 hours.

We then have to deal with the additional 15 minutes and 23 seconds. We could look at 1700 hours, determine the amount of movement of the GP for one hour and divide by the fraction of an hour that 15 minutes and 23 seconds would represent (15 divided by 60 plus 23 divided by 60 =25.383) and we would have the answer, but the almanac has provided an easier way.

Toward the back of the almanac are pages with colored edges. This section is headed "Increments and Corrections". In the upper corners it gives minutes (each page covers two minutes), so find the page that has 15m in the corner.

The first column on the 15m page is seconds and the second column gives the amount of movement of the sun and planets in relation to the number of seconds. Go down that first column to 23, the number of seconds we are looking for, then across you will find 3 50.'8 - that's the distance the GP of the sun traveled in fifteen minutes and twenty-three seconds.

Then we add the 1600 GHA and the 15 23:

GHA 1600 56^0 35.'5
15 23 $+3^0$ 50.'8
Gives us GHA - 1615 23 60^0 26.'3

During the 15 minutes and 23 seconds the sun's latitude changed slightly.

On the daily pages for February 21, 22, 23 under Dec, at the very bottom of the page, is a little "d". We will refer to this as the d factor. In this case the d factor is 0.9, the amount of movement north or south of the GP of the sun during one hour or 1600 to 1700.

The GP of the sun moves south from its most northerly travels, at the summer solstice (which means "sun stands still"), on June 21, 1999 until it reaches the equator on September 23 1999, the autumnal equinox (Equal period of day and night). During this period of time the Dec is decreasing from N 23^0 26.'3 to 0 00.'0, then immediately starts increasing as it continues south.

The GP reaches it's most southern declination on December 22, 1999, the winter solstice, at S 23^0 26.3 then immediately starts moving north, with the numbers decreasing until it reaches the equator, at the vernal equinox. At that point, the numbers increase until the GP is back at its summer solstice.

So, depending on the time of year, the Dec number can be increasing or decreasing. Under our February 21 date you see it is decreasing. When entering Dec write it Dec S 10^0 33.'4 d -0.9, indicating the Dec is decreasing.

Go to the 15m page, the fifth column over labeled "v or d" corrections. Look down that column until you find 0.9, next to it is 0.'2, the distance the sun moved north in 15 minutes and 23 seconds.

Subtract Dec S 10^0 33.'4
 d -0.9 = - 0.'2
Dec 1615 23 S 10^0 33.'2

A review.
Write the exact local time of our sight.
Adjust the local time to UT.
Go to the daily page (sun) for the date.
Write the GHA of the sun for the hour.
Write the Dec of the sun for the hour.
Determine if Dec is increasing or decreasing.
Get the little d factor from the bottom + or -.
Go to the colored pages for minutes and seconds.
Get the d factor from that same page.

It sounds like a lot to remember, but it's very logical and a little practice will hammer it in place.

EXERCISES

Get GHA and Dec for each of the following:
 (1) March 19   (2) October 23   (3) May 22

1632 51 Local   1022 43 Local   1711   41 Local

(4) January 31   (5) November 10   (6) July 7
0915 23 Local   1615 21 Local   1551   51 Local

    You should practice doing this opening the Nautical Almanac only once. Going back and forth to obtain bits of data takes more time and will lead to the possibility of errors.

ANSWERS

(1) March 19
1632 51 Local time
+ 6 Time difference
2232 51 UT

GHA 2200 hr 148^0 03.'5   Dec S 0^0 27.'5 d -1.0
    32 51   + 8 12.'8   - 0.'5
GHA 2232 51 156^0 16.'3 Dec S 0^0 27.'0

(2) October 23
1022 43 Local time
+ 5 Time difference
1522 43 UT

GHA 1500 hr 48^0 54.'4 Dec S 11^0 23.'1 d +0.9
    22 43 +5 40.'8 + 0.'3
GHA 1522 43 54^0 35.'2 Dec 11^0 23.'4

(3) May 22
1711 41 Local time
+ 5 Time difference
2211 41 UT

GHA 2200 hr. 150^0 50.'2 Dec N 20^0 26.'0 d+0.5
    11 41 + 2^0 55.'3 + 0.'1
GHA 2211 41 153^0 45.'5 Dec N 20^0 26.'1

(4) January 31

0915 23 Local time
+ 6 Time difference
1515 23 UT

    GHA 0900 hr 41^0 39.'0   Dec   S 17^0 23.'5 d-0.7
               15 23   + 3^0 50.'8   − 0.'2
    GHA 0915 23 45^0 29.'8   Dec   S 17^0 23.'3

(5) November 10
1615 21 Local time
+6 Time difference
2215 21 UT (November 11)

    GHA 22 154^0 01.'0   Dec S 17^0 12.'5 d +0.7
            15 21   +3 50.'3   +0.2
    GHA 2215 21 157^0 51'.3   Dec   S 17^0 12.'7

(6) July 7
1551 51 Local time
+5 Time difference
2051 51 UT

    GHA 2000 118^0 46.'7   Dec N 22^0 33.'9 d -0.'3
            51 51   + 12^0 57.'8   - 0.'3
    GHA 2051 51 131^0 44.'5   Dec   N 22^0 33.'6

CHAPTER 16

LHA

LHA means Local Hour Angle or the angular distance between your position and the GP of the sun, measured westward from your position.

In Chapter 3 when you have found the GHA of the sun for sight and have corrected your sextant sight from Hs to Ho, you have all the information necessary to deduce a line of position. With the Chapter 3 information, a good understanding of Trigonometry, several pencils and a lot of paper you can obtain your line of position.

Many nineteenth century sea captains were doing this very accurately using British Admiralty Charts, based on surveys done around 1880.

Another method to reduce sights uses a scientific calculator. However, a calculator, which runs on batteries puts me in the same vulnerable position as a GPS without power.

A preferred option is the use of the sight reduction tables, Publications 229 and 249. Pub. 229 is more precise and requires more books. Pub. 249 only has declinations 0 to 29, while 229 covers 0 to 90. Pub. 249 although lacking the precision of 229, is adequate for small boats.

The Ageton method, which uses table 35, from Volume II of Bowditch is slower and requires more math.

Pub. 249 contains the pre-calculation of locations in relation to the GP of a celestial body. Pre-calculation of all possible locations would require a book the size of the Houston Astrodome. To reduce this volume several short cuts have been taken.

Only half the earth was used, the equator to the pole. This takes the position that one half of the earth is the mirror image of the other half. Therefore the pre-calculation of a position in the northern half will duplicate the same position in the southern half. Only whole number LHAs and whole number Decs are given

To find a line of position using the sight reduction tables you must have:

(1) Whole number LHAs.
(2) whole number Decs.
(3) Assumed even latitude.
(4) And to know if you are in the same half of the world as the celestial object.

To explain LHA, I want to return to GHA or Greenwich Hour Angle. This is the longitude of a celestial body, with one small difference: Longitude is counted from Greenwich at 0 degrees westward to the International Date Line at 180 degrees, then counts down to 0 again. So we have longitudes 0 - 180 west and longitudes 180 - 0 east. GHA is counted from 0 at Greenwich all the way around the world back to Greenwich which is 360 degrees (and 0 degrees).

Look at the earth from above the North Pole and draw a line from that pole, down through Greenwich, England to the South Pole. We know that line is longitude zero. Then draw a line from the North Pole through the GP of the sun to the South Pole. This is the longitude of the GP of the sun and is, also, the GHA of the sun or the angle between Greenwich and the GP.

If your longitude position is 92 degrees, and the sun's GP is 200 degrees, which is west of your position, the LHA of the sun is 108.

GHA 200^0
　Your position $\underline{-92^0}$
LHA 108^0

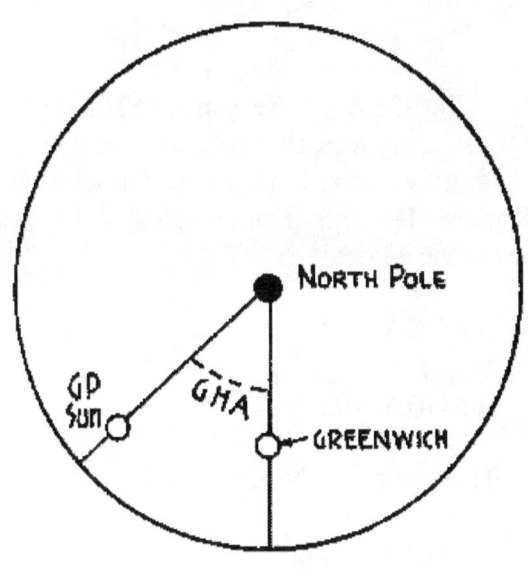

Figure 4-1

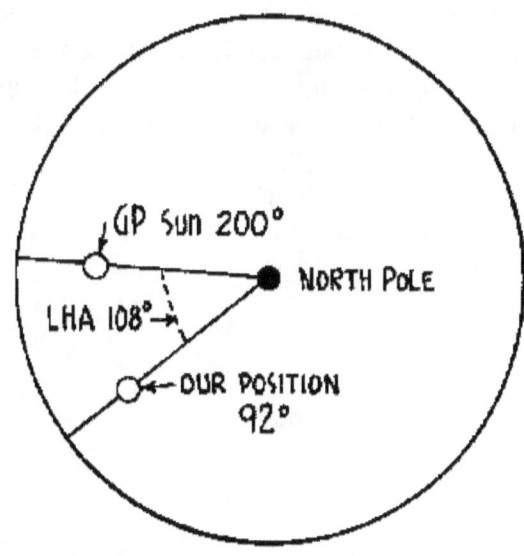

Figure 4-2

If the GHA of the sun is 42 degrees and your position is 92 degrees, the sun is east of you. To measure the angle, go westward, all the way around the world, to 42 degrees. Do this mathematically by adding 360 degrees to the 42 degrees:

sun GHA 42^0
           $+360^0$
sun GHA 402^0

Then we can subtract our 92^0

sun GHA 402^0
Our position $- 92^0$
LHA 310^0

This is the angular distance between your position and the Sun's GP, measured westward from your position.

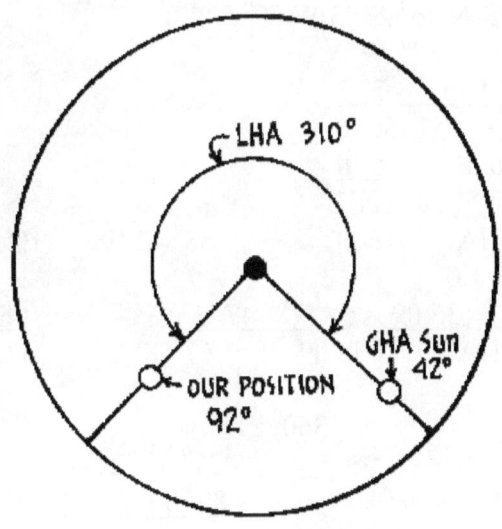

Figure 4-3

An exactly even position rarely occurs, so you create an assumed position. For instance, if your position is 92^0 05.'8 and the GHA of the sun is 156^0 21.'9 and you subtract your position from the GHA, you would have an LHA of 64^0 16.'1. Instead assume your position is 92^0 21.9, which subtracted from the GHA gives an even LHA of 64^0, needed to find the solution in the sight reduction tables.

The difference in plotting from a DR (Dead Reckoning) position to an assumed position is so small, it is of no consequence, as will be the latitude assumption:

If your DR latitude position is 29^0 42.'5, your assumed latitude is 30 degrees. In plotting, note your DR in one place on the chart and your assumed longitude and latitude position in a different place on the chart.

Let's go through the entire procedure for March 28, 1999. Local time 1035 09 UT 1635 09

LL
DR N 26^0 23.'3 W 89^0 50.'3
Hs 57^0 59.'3
8' Dip   - 2.'7
Ha 57^0 56.'6
Main   +15.'6
Ho 58^0 12.'2

GHA	1600	58^0 42.'9	Dec. N 2^0 59.'2 d+1.0
	35 09	+8^0 47.'3	d + .'6
GHA	1635 09	67^0 30.'2	Dec. N 2^0 59.'8
		+360^0	
GHA		427^0 30.'2	
APLo		- 89^0 30.'2	Assumed Pos. Long.
LHA		338^0	APLa 26^0.

An assumed longitude position was subtracted from GHA resulting in a whole number LHA of 338^0. An assumed latitude position of 26^0 was used as it is closest to our DR latitude.

The purpose here is to learn to use Pub. 249, Volume II. The upper corners of each page show LAT and a number. Turn to the pages that show LAT 26^0, which is your APLa (Assumed Position Latitude).

There are several LAT 26^0s so you need to find one that corresponds to our situation. The sun at the time of the sighting was at N 2^0 59.'8, which means your DR is in the same half of the world as the sun. Therefore, you are in the SAME NAME section. Had the sun's GP been south of the equator you would use CONTRARY NAME.

On the side of each page you will see DECLINATION and the inclusive numbers that page covers. Looking for a declination of 2^0 59.'8, find the page that shows LAT 26, SAME NAME and DECLINATIONS (0-14).

On the bottom and top edge of the page are LHA headings. Follow the bottom column down to 336, your LHA.

Then reading across the page to the 2 degree column you will find:

Hc	d	Z
58^0 01	+46	135^0

The d can be plus or minus and doesn't repeat on every number.

Hc is the calculated height of the sighting. If you were at the assumed position and Dec was exactly 2^0, which it's not, you must adjust for the 59.'8 (from the 2^0 59.'8).

The d factor is used for this adjustment. Go to the last page of the sight reduction tables to the page labeled TABLE 5, with a side and top column.

It doesn't matter which number goes in which column, so look in one column for 44 and the other column for 59.8 (the 60 column will be most appropriate). At the junction of these two columns is the answer, in this case 44.

Hc	d	Z
58^0 01	+46	135^0
+44		
58^0 45 Hc (calculated height)		

Enter these numbers on the same paper with the other sight reduction information. The Z 135^0 is equal to

Zn 135^0 which is the exact true heading from your assumed position to the GP of the sun. In the northern hemisphere, if the LHA is greater than 180^0, then Zn = Z. If the LHA is less than 180^0 the true heading would be 360^0- Z = Zn. This information is in the corner of each page.

Now you bring down the Hc 58^0 12.'2 and subtract the smaller of either Hc or Ho.

In this case:

Hc 57^0 45
Ho -58^0 12.'2
          32.'8 mark this A (Away)

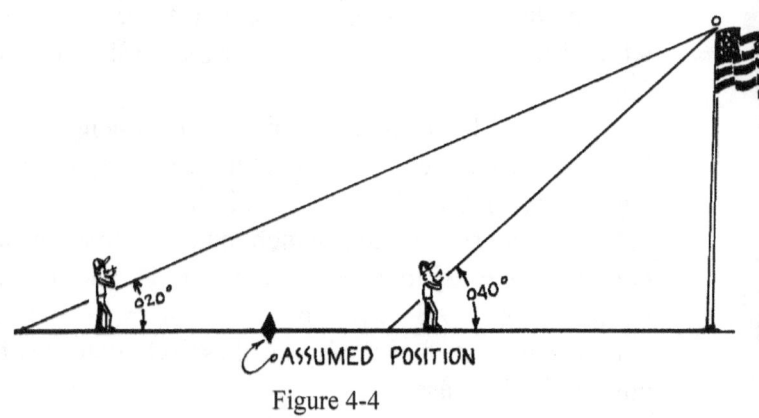

Figure 4-4

The little man is you with your sextant, the closer you get to the flag pole the larger your sextant angle becomes. The further away you are from the flag pole, the smaller the angle.

PLOTTING THE SIGHT

On your chart draw a line from your assumed position out the Zn Line i.e 132 degrees. Then measure

14.8 miles from your AP on the 132 degree line (away the sun). That is your line of position and is drawn perpendicular to the 132 degree line. The distance from AP to LOP is marked (a) below and is called the "altitude intercept" line.

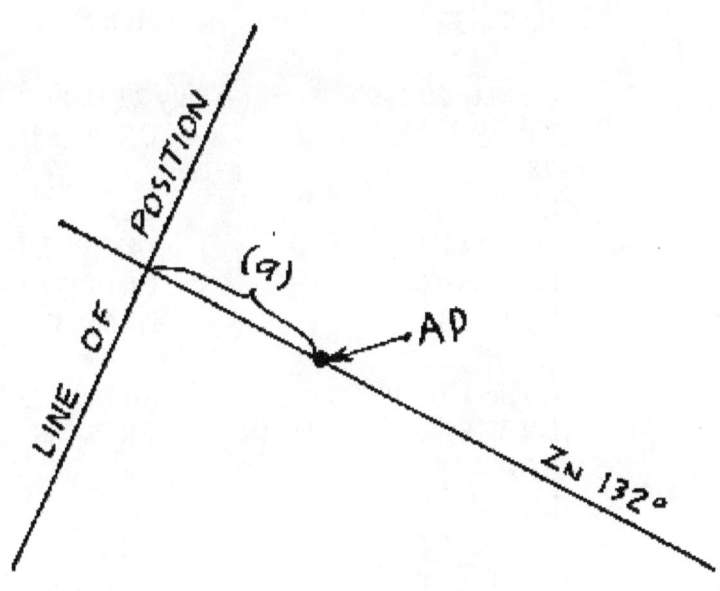

Figure 4-5

EXERCISES

(1) February 20, 1999
DR W $87°$ 43.'8 N $23°$ 56.'9
LL
1555 23 LT
Ht. of eye 8'
Hs $23°$ 36.'8

(2) March 30, 1999
DR W $89°$ 25,'4 N $28°$ 35.'3
UL
0958 52 LT
Ht. of eye 10'
Hs $47°$ 56.'3

(3) May 20 1999
DR W$88°$ 05.'3 N $29°$ 15.'2
LL
1654 54 LT
Ht. of eye 6'
Hs $27°$ 38.'3

(4) July 27 1999
DR W $88°$ 40.'3 N 2939.'8
LL
1432 26 LT
Ht. of eye 8'
Hs $66°$ 42.'1

(5) Sept. 07 1999
DR W $89°$ 23.'6 N $24°$ 16.'1
LL
1021 45 LT
Ht. of eye 8'
Hs $48°$ 25.'8

(6) Nov. 28 1999
DR W $88°$ 23.'5 N $25°$ 45.'9
LL
1556 34 LT
Ht. of eye 21'
Hs $12°$ 34'.5

(7) Dec. 5, 1999
DR E $90°$ 02.'2 S $24°$ 11.'5
LL
0933 45
Ht. of eye 8'
Hs $58°$ 29.'1

(The instruction to subtract an assumed position from GHA that is close to your DR and will give an even

LHA holds true in the entire Western Hemisphere. After crossing the 180 degree International Date Line, instead of subtracting an assumed position, add an assumed position that will round off the LHA).

ANSWERS

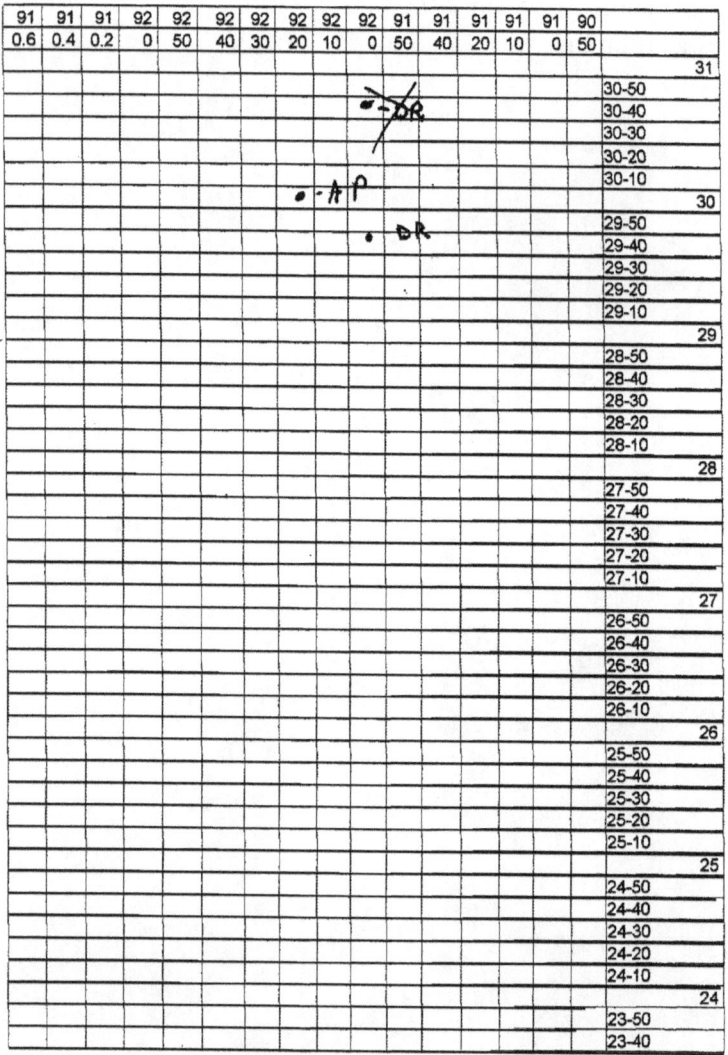

Captain Jack's Complete Navigation, By Jack I. Davis

90	90	89	89	89	89	89	89	88	88	88	88	88	88	87	87	
10	0	50	40	30	20	10	0	50	40	30	20	10	0	50	40	

```
                                                                        30
        2-20-99 LL                                              29-50
        DR W 87 43.'8 N23 56.'9                                 29-40
        LT 1515 23 +6 2155 23 UT                                29-30
 (1) Hs  23 36.'8                                               29-20
 8' Dip   -2.7                                                  29-10
     Ha  23 34.'1                                                     29
 LLMain  +14.'1                          d 0.9                  28-50
     Ho  23 48.'2    GHA (21) 131 34.'1  S 10 50.'6             28-40
                         55 23  13 50.8      -0.'8              28-30
                         GHA   145 24.'9 S 10 49.'6             28-20
                         ApLO   88 24.'9                        28-10
                         LHA    57      ApLA 24                       28
                                        360                     27-50
                    Hc 24 46  -33        -115                   27-40
                          -26           Zn 245                  27-30
                    Hc 24 20                                    27-20
                    Ho 23 48.'2                                 27-10
                         31.'8 A                                      27
                                                                26-50
```

(Plot with Sun line, Ap, DR, and bearing 245)

Page 177

Captain Jack's Complete Navigation, By Jack I. Davis

90	90	89	89	89	89	89	89	88	88	88	88	88	88	87	87	
10	0	50	40	30	20	10	0	50	40	30	20	10	0	50	40	

Plot markings on grid:
- AP (upper left area near 89-20 / 29-10)
- DR (center, near 89-00 / 28-20)
- 126° (azimuth line with arrow)

Right-side latitude scale (top to bottom): 30, 29-50, 29-40, 29-30, 29-20, 29-10, 29, 28-50, 28-40, 28-30, 28-20, 28-10, 28, 27-50, 27-40, 27-30, 27-20, 27-10, 27, 26-50, 26-40, 26-30, 26-20, 26-10, 26, 25-50, 25-40, 25-30, 25-20, 25-10, 25, 24-50, 24-40, 24-30, 24-20, 24-10, 24, 23-50, 23-40, 23-30, 23-20, 23-10, 23, 22-50, 22-40

Handwritten work:

(2) 3-30-99 UL
DR W 89 25.'4 N 28 35.'3
Local time 0948 52 +6 1558 52 UT

Hs   52 01.'9
10' Dip   –3.'1
Ha   51 58.'8
UL main   16.'9
Ho   51 36.'3   GHA ((15) 43 51.'8   N 3 45.'9   + 1.'0
Hc   51 16   58 52   14 43.'0   – 1.'0
         20.'3 T   58 34.'8   N 3 46.'9
                                           +360
                                           418 34.'8
                                   ApLO   89 34.'8   ApLA 29
                                   LHA   329

                                   Hc 50 43 –42   Zn 126
                                        + 33
                                   Hc 51 16

Page 178

Captain Jack's Complete Navigation, By Jack I. Davis

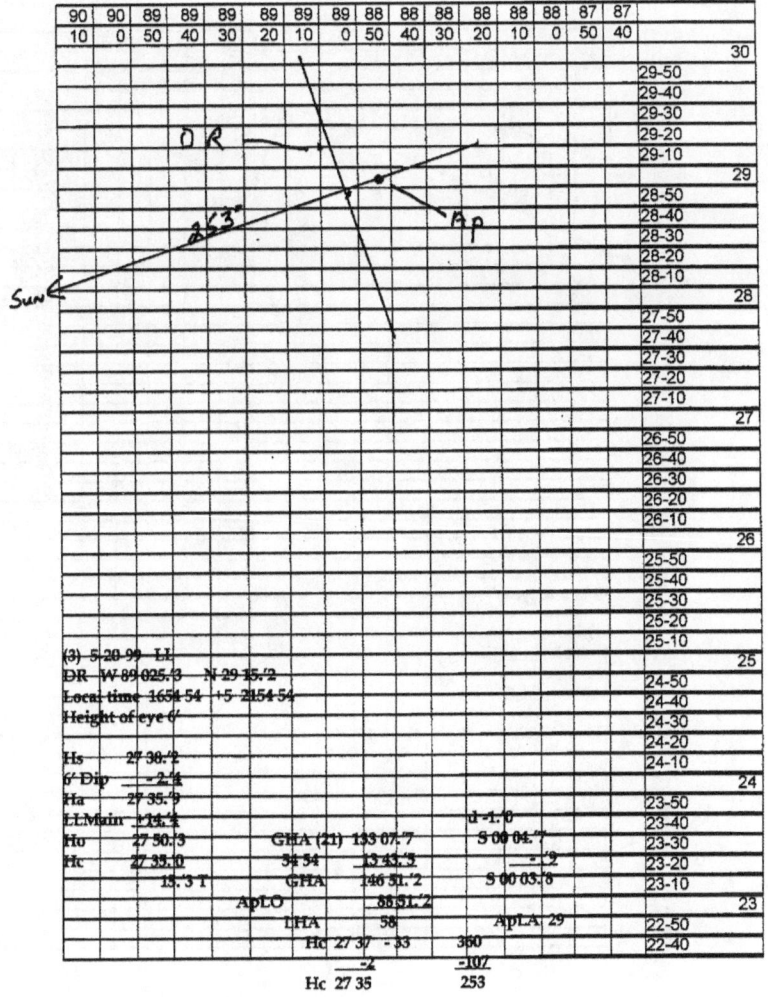

Page 179

Captain Jack's Complete Navigation, By Jack I. Davis

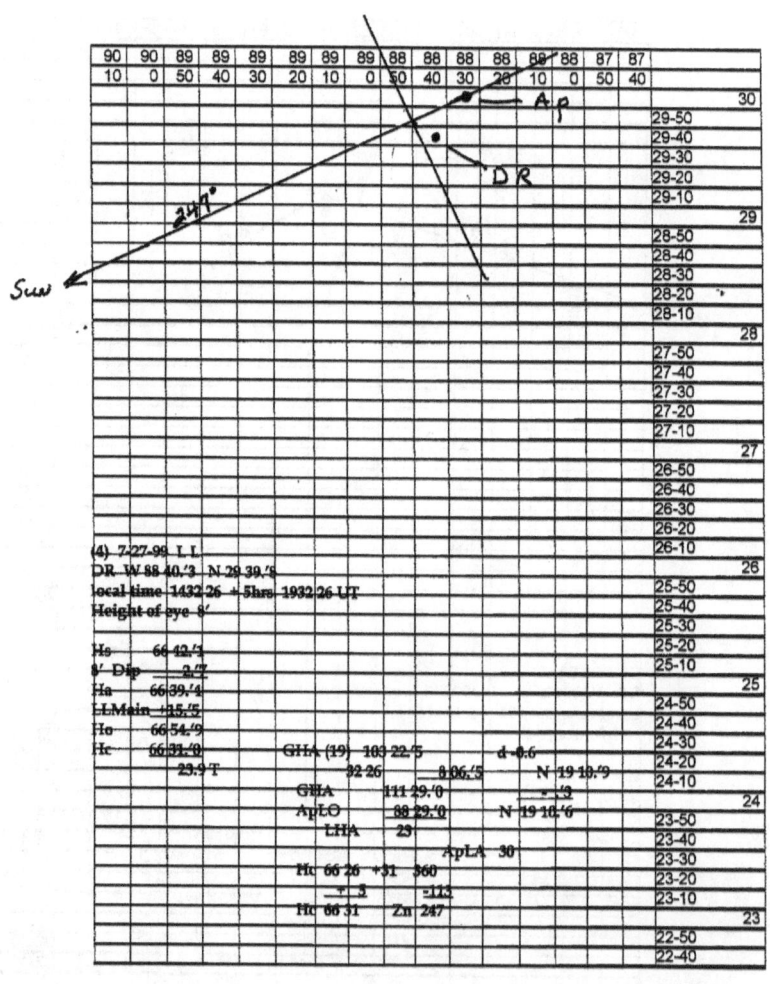

Captain Jack's Complete Navigation, By Jack I. Davis

90	90	89	89	89	89	89	89	88	88	88	88	88	88	87	87	
10	0	50	40	30	20	10	0	50	40	30	20	10	0	50	40	
																30
																29-50
(5) 9-7-99	L L															29-40
DR W 89	23.'6	N 24	16.'1													29-30
Local time	1021	45	+ 5hrs	1521	45 UT											29-20
Height of eye 8'																29-10
																29
Hs	48 25.'8															28-50
8' Dip	-2.'7															28-40
Ha	48 23.'1															28-30
LLmain	+15.'1															28-20
Ho	48 38.'2	GHA (15)	45 25.'7		d -0.9											28-10
		21 45	5 26.'3		N 6 05.'0											28
		GHA	50 55.'0		- 3											27-50
		+360			N 6 05.'0											27-40
		410 55.'0														27-30
		ApLO	88 55.'0		ApLA 24											27-20
		LHA	322													27-10
Hc 49 20	+30	Z= 110														27
+ 2																26-50
Hc 49 22																26-40
Ho 48 38.'2																26-30
43.'8 A																26-20
																26-10

Captain Jack's Complete Navigation, By Jack I. Davis

(6) LL 11-28-99
DR W 88 23.'5 W 25 45.'9
Local time 1556 34 +6hrs. 2156 34
Height of eye 21'

Hs	12 34.'5
21'Dip	-4.'5
Ha	12 30.'0
LLmain	+12.'0
Ho	12 42.'0
Hc	12 30.'0
	12.'0 T

GHA (21) 138 00.'7   d +0.'4
    56 34   14 08.'5   S 21 20.'2
  GHA   152 09.'2   +.'5
ApLo   88 09.'2   S 21 20.'7
    LHA 64   ApL A 25
Hc 12 41 -.31 360
       -.11   -12
Hc 12 30   Zn 239

Plot annotations: DR, AP, 23°, Sun

Right-side scale (degrees and minutes):
30
29-50
29-40
29-30
29-20
29-10
29
28-50
28-40
28-30
28-20
28-10
28
27-50
27-40
27-30
27-20
27-10
27
26-50
26-40
26-30
26-20
26-10
26
25-50
25-40
25-30
25-20
25-10
25
24-50
24-40
24-30
24-20
24-10
24
23-50
23-40
23-30
23-20
23-10
23
22-50
22-40

Top scale: 90 90 | 89 89 89 | 89 89 89 | 88 88 88 | 88 88 88 | 87 87
           10 0 | 50 40 30 | 20 10 0 | 50 40 30 | 20 10 0 | 50 40

Captain Jack's Complete Navigation, By Jack I. Davis

90	90	89	89	89	89	89	89	88	88	88	88	88	88	87	87		
10	0	50	40	30	20	10	0	50	40	30	20	10	0	50	40		
																	30
																29-50	
																29-40	
(7) 12-5-99 L L																29-30	
DR E 90 02.'2 S 24 11.'5																29-20	
Local time 0923 45 -6hrs = 0333 45																29-10	
Height of eye 8'																	29
																28-50	
Hs 58 29.'1																28-40	
8' Dip - 2.'7																28-30	
Ha 58 26.'4																28-20	
LLMain + 15.'6																28-10	
Ho 58 42.'0																	28
							GHA (03) 227 25.'5				d +0.'3					27-50	
							33 45	8 26.'3			S 22 17.'7					27-40	
							GHA	235 51.'8			+ .2					27-30	
						ApLO	90 08.'2			S 22 17.'9						27-20	
						LHA 326										27-10	
										ApLA 24							27
Hc 58 43 +10 180																26-50	
: 3 - 87																26-40	
Hc 58 46 Zn 093																26-30	
Ho 58 42																26-20	
↑ A																26-10	
																	26

Page 183

CHAPTER 17

STARS AND PLANETS

To better understand Ho-Hc, altitude intercept and LOPs, note that the solution (the line of position) is actually the distance away from the GP, and is not a straight line, but a circle going all the way around the GP.

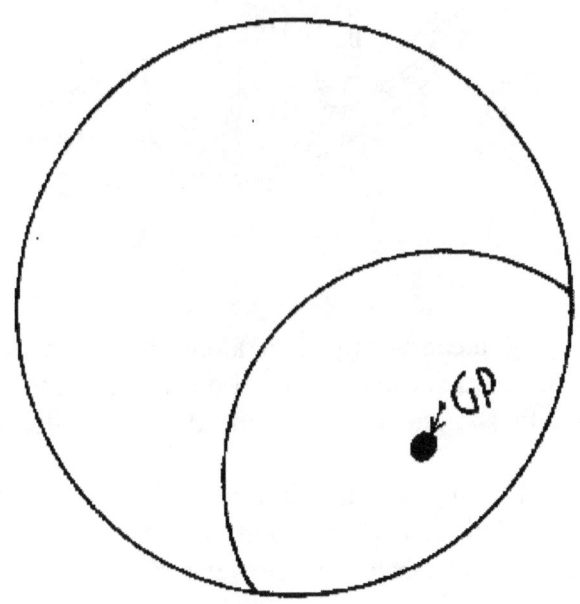

Figure 5-1

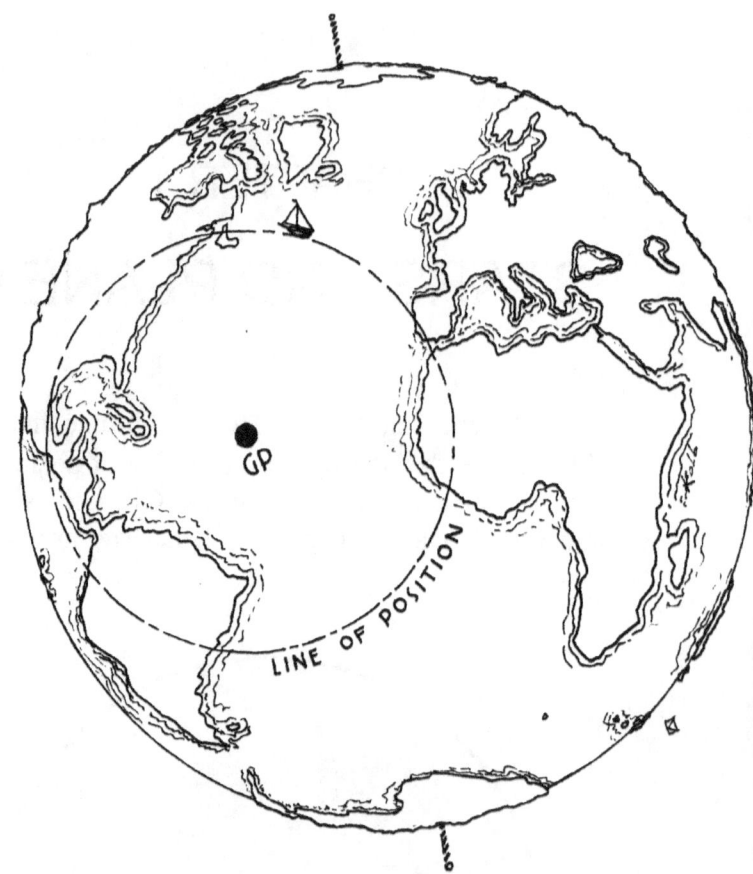

Figure 5-2

You can be anywhere along this circle. In reality, the circles are so huge that on our charts these lines are virtually straight and everyone draws them as straight lines.

I don't use my navigation charts for plotting because they cost so much and I hate to mark them up, so I use plotting sheets 969. However there is no objection to using Universal Plotting sheets. I don't use the Universal Plotting sheets because I can't seem to get the accuracy I would like, probably due to the small chart size.

Some navigators put little value in one LOP (line of position), for instance a sun sight alone. But keep in mind that a sun sight early in the day, when the Zn is about 90 degrees, gives you a good longitude position. Then at noon, even if you don't pin down the exact time of meridian passage (exact local noon) to establish your precise longitude, your latitude position will be correct for a time window of several minutes.

Again in late evening, when the Zn of the sun is at about 270 degrees, you have another good longitude fix.

This is not as dependable as a fix of three different bodies, taken at about the same time and in different directions, such as three stars or a planet and two stars or the Moon, a planet and a star, but keep in mind that you can navigate around the world using nothing but sun sights.

Many newcomers to ocean navigation using GPS or Loran fix their position on the chart as often as once per hour. If a dot was put on a chart of the Gulf of Mexico that often, they would be connecting the dots, which accomplishes very little.

The success of navigation using a sextant, depends on how well you maintain a DR (Dead Reckoning) position, when a single line of position, as well as a three-body fix, confirms your position.

PLANETS

There is one small difference between working a planet sight and a sun sight. Find March 8,9,10 in the daily pages. On the left in the second column is "Venus - 4.0". At the bottom of the column is a "d" factor of 1.3, which is used the same as a sun sight, Go down the Dec column to determine if the numbers are increasing or decreasing. In this case they are increasing, so label it "d. + 1.3 and adjust the Dec accordingly.

There is also a "v" next to the "d". This is an additional correction to GHA, (the "d" is under the Dec column and the "v" is under the GHA column). It will always be plus unless labeled otherwise. Find the correct adjustment in the color pages at the back of the almanac, using the same columns as the "d" adjustment.

Brightness of the planets (and stars) is expressed in numbers, with brighter stars being zero. As the object gets dimmer the number increases. In the case of objects brighter than a bright star the expression is with a minus, the bigger the minus number the brighter the object. (Sirius at -1.6 and Canopus at -0.9 are far brighter than most stars). This method also applies to other celestial bodies such as comets.

On the March 8,9,10 page, Venus is shown as -4.0, which is the brightest object in the sky except the sun and Moon. (Venus can get as bright as -4.4. The moon varies to -12.6 and the sun at -26.7).

Some publications show stars by "first magnitude", "second magnitude", etc. All stars with a magnitude of 1.5 or better are classified as first magnitude; 1.51 to 2.5 are second magnitude; 2.51 to 3.5 are third magnitude; 3.51 to 4.5 are fourth magnitude; 4.51 to 5.5 are fifth magnitude; and 5.51 to 6.5 are sixth magnitude.

Venus can be seen during daylight hours if you know where to look. By working the sight ahead of time you can find it by setting your sextant to the predicted altitude facing the Zn direction. If you can't find it through your sextant scope, try looking for it with a good pair of binoculars.

The top of the page next to Venus reads "Mars - 0.4." Mars is not as bright as Venus, but is slightly brighter than most bright stars.

Jupiter is -2.1, extremely bright, and Saturn, at +.5, is only slightly dimmer than the brighter stars.

Twilight is the best time to take a planet sight.

The Nautical Almanac gives morning and evening twilight times. On the March 8,9,10 pages, find Twilight and beneath that heading is Naut. (for Nautical) and Civil. Nautical twilight is the very beginning of twilight. The sun is down, but it's still light enough to see the horizon and the first of the brightest stars and planets begin to appear to the naked eye.

Civil twilight is the end of the twilight period. The horizon is no longer visible, even though there may be a little leftover light toward the west.

These twilight periods occur at different times, depending on the latitude. Go down the column to the latitude nearest your DR, and use N. 30 degrees. On the 30 degree line is 0526, the beginning of Nautical twilight, and 0554 for Civil twilight.

This is the twilight time frame for Greenwich, England. It will also be the correct time each hour moving west, but only if you are in the exact center of the time zone. In Houston we are at 92^0 55 which is 2 degrees 55 minutes past the center of our time zone. We can make an adjustment for time by calculating how long it would take for the planet (or sun) to travel 2 degrees, 55 minutes at the westward speed of 900 knots. This is not complicated math, but there's a much easier way.

Use the color pages in the back of the almanac. Look, down the column. Sun and Planets for 2^0 55. It will be at 11 minutes 40 seconds. Add this time to 0526 and 0554. Local twilight time will be:

+11 40 = 0537 40 and 0565 40.

EXERCISES

Try the morning sight for March 9, 1999.
0537 40 local time plus 6 = 1137 40 March 9.

		d +1.'3
GHA (11)	$313°53.'9$	N $7°06.'9$
37 40	$9°25.'0$	+ .'8
v -0.3	-.'2	N $7°07.'7$
GHA	$323°18.'7$	
Aplo	$91°18.'7$	ApLa $29°$
LHA	$232°$	

The Sight Reduction Tables stop before LHA 232. Therefore, the planet is below the horizon at that time.

Now the evening sight for March 9, 1999.

1804   beginning of civil twilight.
   11 40   time adjustment. (from color pages)
+ 600   hours
2415 40 = 0015 40 March 10, 1999

		d +1.'3
GHA (00)	$148°49.'6$	N $7°23.'3$
15 40	$3°55.'0$	+ .'3
v -0.3	-.'1	N $7°23.'6$
GHA	$152°44.'5$	
Aplo	$91°44.'5$	ApLa $29°$
LHA	$61°$	

Hc $28°41$ d +29 $360°$

$$\frac{+12}{Hc\ 28°\ 53} \qquad \frac{Z - 98°}{Zn\ 262°}$$

At 1815 local time, Venus will be 28 degrees 53 minutes above the horizon, on a true heading of 262 degrees. You can then take the sight, note the time and have a good LOP of Venus.

Following across the March 10, 00 UT line you surmise that Mars is below the horizon at that time but Jupiter and Saturn may not be.

Practice the following using the same parameters:

W $92°$ 05 and N $29°$ 00.

March 9, 1999 Jupiter LT 1815 40 + 6 = 0015 40 (March 10)

```
    GHA    161° 32.'6           N 1° 15.'9    d +0.'2
    15 40    3° 55.'0              + .'1
    GHA   165° 27.'6           N 1° 16.'0
    V+1.9    + .'5
    GHA   165° 28.'1
    ApLo   92° 28.'1           ApLA 29°
    LHA    73°

    Hc    15° 19.'0     +30    360°
    +8.'0              -Z 98°
    Hc    15° 27.'0            Zn 262°
```

March 9, 1999 Saturn LT 1815 40 +6 = 0015 40 (March 10)

```
        GHA      137° 38.'9          N 9° 40.'1    d +
0.'1
        15 40     3° 55.'0                    .'0
        GHA  141° 33.'9              N 9° 40.'1
        V + 2.2    +.'6
              141° 34.'5
        ApLo   92° 34.'5             ApLA 29°
        LHA     49°

        Hc      39° 59         +30    360°
             +20               -Z 103°
        Hc      40° 29                Zn 257°
```

STARS

There are so many navigational stars that trickery is required to list a GP for each one. Instead of a GHA for each star, the Nautical Almanac lists a GHA for Aries, which is only a hypothetical place in the sky.

When you have recorded the GHA for Aries, for the hours, minutes and seconds of your sight, add to that number the SHA of the star you chose.

SHA stands for Sidereal Hour Angle, and is the angular distance from the point in the sky called Aries, to the stars GHA. No correction is necessary for Dec because the movement is so slow.

When you add the GHA of Aries, and the SHA of a star, you have to subtract 360 if your answer exceeds that.

EXERCISES

DR W 92^0 06 N 29^0 33

(1) March 10, 1999
Sirius
1829 34 LT
Ht. of eye 10'

(2) August 28. 1999
Betelgeuse
0545 21 LT
Ht. of eye 8'

Captain Jack's Complete Navigation, By Jack I. Davis

ANSWERS

(1) 3-9-99 Sirius
DR W 92^0 06 N 29^0 33
1829 34 LT + 6 = (3-10) 00 29 34 UT

GHA Aries 00 167^0 13.'7
29 34 7^0 24.'7
GHA Aries 174^0 38.'4
SHA Sirius 258^0 43.'3   Dec S 16^0 43.'2
GHA Sirius 433^0 21.'7
ApLO 92^0 21.'7
LHA Sirius 341^0

Hc 41^0 24   -56   Zn 155^0
     - 40
Hc 40^0 44

(2) 8-28-99 Belelgeuse
DR W 92^0 06 W 29^0 33
0545 21 Lt + 5 hours = 1045 21
Ht. of eye 8'

GHA Aries 126^0 11.'0
45 21 11^0 22.'1
GHA Aries 137^0 3 3.'1
SHA Betelgeuse 271^0 13.'0   N 7^0 24.'4
GHA Betelgeuse 408^0 46.'1
ApLO 92^0 46.'1
LHA Betelgeuse 316^0

Hc 43^0 07'   +33   Zn 109^0
   + 13
Hc 43^0 20'

CHAPTER 18

STAR FINDERS

With time and practice, you will learn to identify a great many stars, but you don't have to know the stars to take sextant sights.

You can use a star finder to select the stars to shoot, the direction to face to locate each star and the approximate sextant setting of each star.

The star finder has a star base that shows "north" on one side and "south" on the other. Select the north side and attach that to the 35^0 N latitude template.

Using the example, March 10, 1999, the star Sirius, local time 1819 34 and the DR of W 92^0 06 and N 29^0 33, you will find the GHA of Aries was 173^0 07.'1, which is used with the star finder.

$$173^0\ 07.'1$$
ApLO $\quad 92^0\ 07.'1$
Aries LHA $\quad\quad 81^0$

The lined, blue area on the template represents the visible sky at your location. An arrow runs from the center of the blue area to the numbered edge. Turn the template until the arrow points to 81 degrees.

Following the arrow back to the beginning of the blue area, you will see that the arrow is 180 degrees. Move right to $170°$ then $160°$. Half way to $150°$ is a line representing $155°$.

Follow the $155°$ line toward the center of the blue area. Sirius is close to that line, just above the $35°$ line. The star finder shows Sirius will have a Zn of about $155°$ and an altitude of about $35+°$.

Since you have already worked this sight, you know the actual Zn is $154°$ and the actual sextant sight will be $39°$ 06. The star finder is not perfect, but using the prediction, facing $155°$, and presetting our sextant to $35°$, we could easily find the star.

To the left you will see a star called Hamal at about the $270°$ line, with a height of about $45°$. Further on you will find a star called Regulas, at about the $90°$ line, with a height of about $23°$.

Work these two and see how close the predictions are.

Star Hamal
March 10, 1999
DR W $92°$ 06 N $29°$ 33
local time 1819 34 + 6 = (3-11) 00 19 34 UT

```
GHA 00   168° 12.'8
19 34             4° 54.'3
GHA Aries      173° 07.'1
SHA Hamal      328° 13.'5    N 23° 27.'4
GHA Hamal      501° 20.'6
ApLO            92° 20.'6
         409° 00.'0
       - 360° 00.'0
LHA Hamal       49°

Hc       45° 52        +18    360°
```

$$\text{Hc} \quad \begin{array}{c} +8 \\ \hline 47^0 \ 00 \end{array} \qquad \begin{array}{c} -86^0 \\ \hline \text{Zn } 274^0 \end{array}$$

Our prediction was height of 45^0 and Zn 270^0 so we were close enough.

Star Regulas 3-10-99
DR W 92^0 06 N29^0 33
Local time 1819 34 + 6 hours (3-11) 00 1934

GHA Aries	168^0 12.'8	
19 34	4^0 54.'3	
GHA Aries	173^0 07.'1	
SHA Regulas	207^0 54.'9	N 11^0 58.2
GHA Regulas	381^0 02.'0	
ApLO	92^0 02.'0	
LHA Regulas	289^0	

Hc $\quad 21^0$ 50 $\qquad$ +28 $\quad$ Zn 089^0
$\quad \underline{+26}$
Hc $\quad 22^0$ 16

Our prediction was 90^0 and height 23^0, so this one is fine.

CHAPTER 19

THE MOON

The moon is so close, that special consideration must be given to horizontal parallax (HP), which is a second correction to apparent height (Ha).

The sextant correction tables are in the back of the Nautical Almanac.

The top section, left page covers Ha, from $0°$ through $34°$. The top part right covers Ha $35°$ to $90°$.

On the right page find 48. Beneath this number are the corrections for 48 -- 48 10, 48 20, 48 30, 48 40 and 48 50. Our Ha is $48° 16.9$. which is closest to 48 20 = 48.1. Follow the same column down to the second section, HP, where you have corrections for LL and UL. The lower limb correction is 3.8

All corrections are added, but if it's an upper limb shot, you subtract 30 minutes.

DR W 92^0 00.'0 N 29^0 00.'0
Moon LL 5-22-99 local time 1720 10 + 5 = 2220 10

```
    Hs      48⁰ 20          GHA (22) 48⁰ 16.'1    N 9⁰ 51.'7 d -9.'6
    10' Dip  - 3.'1  20 10      4⁰ 48.'7            -3.'3
    Ha      48⁰ 16.'9       V 12.'7        4.'3   N 9⁰ 48.'4
    Main    +48.'1 Ha       53⁰ 09.'1
    HP 56.3  +3.'8                +360⁰ 00.'0
    Ho      49⁰ 08.'8              413⁰ 09.'1
    Hc      48⁰ 47.'0       ApLO    92⁰ 09.'1
              21.8T    LHA    321⁰


    Hc      48⁰ 21          +33    Zn 110⁰
           +26
    Hc      48⁰ 47
```

CHAPTER 20

THE NOON SIGHT

The noon sight can be learned in a matter of minutes;

(1) Take your sextant sight (at noon) and reduce Hs to Ho.

(2) Subtract your Ho from 90ø.

(3) The remainder is the zenith distance. If you faced south to take the sight, label this remainder N. If you faced north, label it S.

(4) Add or subtract the sun's Dec. If your remainder is labeled N, and the Dec is N, you add. If the signs are different you subtract.

(5) The remainder is your latitude.

However, you must know exactly when noon occurs. If you know your exact longitude local noon can be determined from the nautical almanac by finding the time the GHA of the sun matches your longitude.

At sea, you won't always know your exact longitude, so a different method is needed. If you start checking the altitude of the sun a little before noon, you will see the sun get higher and higher, until it reaches maximum height. It then starts decreasing in height. The problem being, at the maximum height, the sun seems to hang, with several seconds going by before a change occurs.

Local noon occurs some time during this hang period, which doesn't give you a definite time.

A reliable method is to get a good sight a few minutes before local noon, record the time and wait for the sun to reach its maximum height. Watch through your sextant for the sun to get back to your earlier sight height. Record the exact time the sun reaches that point. Local noon will have occurred precisely halfway between the first and last recorded times.

If you get the time exactly right, you will have a "fix". Your longitude will be the same as the sun's GHA, (the LHA is zero) Take the GHA directly from the nautical almanac and that is your longitude. Determine your latitude with the five-step method given above. You don't need sight reduction tables for either.

EXERCISES

(1) DR W92^0 00.'0 N 29^0 00.'0
May 25, 1999
Star - Alphecca
1850 30 local time
Ht. of eye 8'
Hs 16^0 50.'9

(2)
May 25,1999
Moon
1850 30 local time
Ht. of eye 8'
Hs 32^0 39.'6

(3) DR W 92^0 00.'0 N 29^0 00.'0
May 25, 1999
Venus
1851 30 local time
Ht. of eye 8'
Hs 55^0 41.'8

(4) DR W88^0 15.'2 N 28^0 15.'3
May 1, 1999
Time - morning twilight
Ht of eye 8'

Altair	Antares	Spica
Hs 56^0 59.8	Hs 31^0 24.'3	Hs 13^0 58.'6

ANSWERS

(1) May 25, 1999
Star Alphecca
1850 30 local time +5 hours = 2350 30
Ht of eye 8'

Hs	16^0 50.'9
Dip 8'	-2.'7
Ha	16^0 48.'2
Main	-3.'2
Ho	16^0 45.'0
Hc	-16^0 37.'0
	8' T

Aries (23)	228^0 04.'9	
50 30	12^0 39.'6	
GHA Aries	240^0 44.'5	
SHA Alphecca	126^0 19.'9	N 26^0 43.'1
GHA Alphecca	367^0 04.'4	
ApLO	92^0 04.'4	

LHA   275⁰   ApLA 29

Hc   16⁰ 19   +25   Zn 069
    +18
Hc   16⁰ 37

(2) DR 92^0 00 N 29^0 00
May 25, 1999
LL Moon 1850 30 local time +5 hours = 2350 30
Ht of eye 8'

Hs	32^0 39.'6				
Dip 8'	-2.'8				
Ha	32^0 36.'8				
Hp 54.5	+1.'5				
Main	+57.'7				
d +10.'3					
Ho	3^0 36.'0	GHA	30^0	45.'3	
S 2^0 35.'8					
Hc	33^0 22.'0	50 30	12^0	03.'0	
+ 8.'7					
	14 T	V15.'1	12.'7	S 2^0 44.'5	

GHA 43^0 01.'0
      360^0 00.'0
      403^0 01.'0
ApLO -92^0 01.'0
LHA 311^0

ApLA 29

Hc   33 49   -37   Zn = 115
   -27
Hc   33 22

(3) DR W 92⁰ 00 N 29⁰ 00
May 25, 1999
Venus 1851 30 local time + 5 Hours = 2351 30
Ht of eye 8'

```
Hs        55⁰ 41.'8
Dip 8'    - 2.'7
Ha        55⁰ 39.'1
Ex        + 0.'1
Main      - 0.'7
     d -0.'4
Ho        55⁰ 38.'5      GHA (23)    117⁰  20.'2
   N24⁰ 46.'7
                         51 30       12⁰ 52.'5
-0.'3
                         V -0.4             -0.'3    N24⁰
46.'4
                         GHA         130⁰ 12.'4
                         ApLO         92⁰ 12.'4
                         LHA              38

Hc        55 46          +17   360
   +13                    89
Hc        55 59          Zn = 271
- Ho      55 38.'5
          20.'5 A
```

(4) May 1, 1999
Twilight 0421 - 6 59 minutes = 041401 + 5 hours = 091401
Ht of eye 8'

51.'0

30.'8

21.'8
    Aries GHA 353^0
    14 01 3^0
              357^0

Altair
GHA Aries 357^0 21.'8   dec N 8^0 51.'9
SHA Altair 62^0 18.'8   ApLA 28^0
GHA Altair 419^0 40.'6   Hs 56^0 59.'8
ApLo 88^0 40.'6   Dip
            -2.'7
LHA   331   Ha 56^0 57.'1
                               Main   - 0.'6
Hc   56 06   +38   Zn = 121   Ho 56^0 56.'5
       +33   Hc 56^0 39.'0
Hc   56 39
       17.'5 T

Antares

GHA Aries 357^0 21.'8
SHA Antares 112^0 39.'4
            470^0 00.'2   Hs 31^0 24.'3
ApLO 88^0 00.'2   Dip -2.'7
LHA   382   Ha 31^0 21.'6
          - 360   Main - 1.'6
LHA   22   Ho 31^0 20.'0

Hc $32^0\ 00$ -55 360
       -24 157
Hc $31^0\ 36$ Zn 203
Ho $31^0\ 20$
       16A

Spica
May 1, 99
Twilight 0421 - 6 59= 041401 + 5 hours = 0914 01
DR W 88^0 15.'2 N 28^0 15.'3

GHA Aires 357^0 21.'8
SHA Spica 158^0 42.'5
      516^0 04.'3   dec S 11^0 09.'5
ApLO 88^0 04.'3   ApLA 28^0
             428
             -360 Hs 13^0 58.'6
LHA   68   Dip $-$ 2.'7

                                    Ha 13^0 55.'9
                                    Main $-3.'8$
Hc 13^0 36 -33 360   Ho 13^0 52.'1
       -6 -111 Hc 13^0 30
Hc 13^0 30   Zn 249
22.'1 T

BOATING STORIES

Captain Jack's Complete Navigation, By *Jack I. Davis*

PREFACE

A friend brought up the fact that I deliver boats. He questioned how I determined an unknown boat is seaworthy just by looking around. "It would take me forever to check it out and even then I would be afraid that I had missed something." he said.

It's not quite that simple, and yet in a way it is. My experience of checking hundreds of boats has given me a certain amount of confidence.

However, my ability to discern well hidden, potential problems on a prospective delivery is no better than anyone's. In these situations, my salvation was not in finding the problems ahead of time, but resolving the problems once they surfaced.

The ability to solve these problems is the product of years of experiencing situations, in which mind-boggling, confidence-questioning disasters occurred on a regular basis. Many times, solving problems has nothing to do with ability, but is just plain luck.

The following, from my various logs, is a compilation of some of these near disasters, my reactions to them, and how the problems were resolved, if indeed, they were resolved.

Captain Jack's Complete Navigation, By Jack I. Davis

RIGGING PROBLEMS

My first Gulf Stream crossing as the captain of a sailboat, started from an anchorage close to Key Largo in Florida. My destination was Bimini, in the Bahamas, not more than an overnight sail away.

Leaving at dusk on this kind of crossing is common because it will be daylight before you reach shallow water and the islands.

On this trip, the evening was perfect for sailing. The wind was southeast at about fifteen knots, the seas were moderate, and with a completely cloudless sky. The little thirty-five foot sloop was charging through the phosphorescent seas like a freight train.

Most people can only dream of having an experience this beautiful. In fact, my dreams got me into this lifestyle and were as romantically exquisite.

I had carefully plotted the course to Bimini, taking into consideration the estimated speed of the Gulf Stream and its effect on my sailing plan. The stream can have a velocity of three or four knots (or more) in the center but from the center to the edges, that velocity drops to zero, or turns around as a counter current. You have to estimate average speed but when doing that, your DR (dead reckoning) can be off. In those days I had no electronic aids, but in daylight and with crystal clear water the approach seemed safe.

My DR position at midnight had me at about the middle of the Gulf Stream. With everything going well, I decided to go below and nap for an hour or so, leaving a capable crew at the helm.

It was a moderately cool night and I was wearing a light jacket with my safety harness on over it as I lay on my bunk. At sea, and especially at night, this is standard procedure.

No more than thirty minutes later there was a loud thump on deck.

I flipped on the spreader lights as I raced out on deck. The lower port shrouds had come loose from the mast and had fallen on deck. The mast was flexing, bending an enormous amount, giving the impression that it would snap at any second.

I secured my harness to the jackline, ran forward, dropped the jib and the mainsail, but this did not stop the flexing. I had never planned on anything like this and, in fact, had never heard of shrouds falling off. I got the jib halyard and flipped it around the mast just below the spreaders, then brought it down to the opposite toe rail and secured it. I was then able to winch the halyard down, thereby damping the flexing.

Since that maneuver seemed to work, I did the same with the main halyard, going the opposite way around the mast. After winching that down, the flexing slowed to an acceptable amount. Then I sat down and wondered how in the hell I knew to do that.

I rested long enough to get my pulse under control and to decide what to do next. I didn't know the reason for the failure or what I would need in the way of equipment to resolve the problem. But whatever I would need, it probably would not be available in the Bahamas. It became obvious I needed to go back to Florida.

I changed course and motored in the general direction of Florida. I got my charts out and tried to estimate about where I would end up in Florida. However, the velocity of the Gulf Stream being so variable, I could do little more than guess. A sailor accustomed to sailing the east coast of Florida could recognize some landmark. Having never been to this part of the world, I knew I had very little chance of pinpointing my position by landmarks.

My DR at the time of the course change was very iffy. When you plot a course, that plot is in doubt if you don't know where you are leaving from.

The next best thing was to get close enough to Florida to see, and time one or more navigation lights to establish a position. On the east coast of Florida there are lights at variable intervals spaced along the barrier reef that separates Florida from the Gulf Stream. Spotting them is a major challenge since there are millions of lights onshore and marine navigation lights tend to blend in with the other lights.

I got out my stop watch and binoculars, and as soon as I got close enough I started spotting and timing. The tension was incredible, because a very unforgiving reef lay between me and the mainland. Without establishing a position on the chart, the little sailboat could become a permanent addition to the reef system. After what seemed like ages, I spotted a blinking white, five-second light that appeared on the chart at a reasonable place.

I began to relax a little after I thought my position was fixed, and with the autopilot singing away, I watched the white five-second light get closer.

Suddenly, out of the corner of my eye, I spotted an object close to the starboard side of the boat! Before I could get to the autopilot the boat passed a green intra-coastal channel marker. I had already crossed the reef and I was crossing the ICW.

I disengaged the autopilot, continued on just far enough to clear the channel and dropped anchor. I poured a medium- sized glass of scotch, and kicked back to try to unwind, while I continued to watch the five-second light.

The next morning, after a night's rest, I awoke to find what I thought was a five second marine navigation light, was a light on a McDonalds's restaurant. I could almost hear Ronald laughing.

I contemplated this development over breakfast of bacon, eggs, hash browns, biscuits and cream gravy. I like to eat well when I'm at sea, (and when I'm ashore). I got the charts and fixed my position by checking the still visible ICW marker on the chart. With that information I found the approximate place I crossed the reef but there wasn't a place to cross. Sailing and navigational ability are very important assets, but luck is better.

The problem with the shroud turned out to be very simple. We had recently put all new rigging on the boat, using Sta-lock fittings. I rigged the lower shrouds on the starboard side of the mast, putting the shroud fitting between the two tangs attached to the mast, then putting a clevis pin through with a cotter key.

The port side was rigged by my associate, who put the two tangs together, then put the clevis pin through, then the shroud fitting, which is wrong. I didn't check it, so I have to take the blame. If you were to check this fitting from the deck it would look all right, but you would have to go up the mast to discover that it was improperly installed. This incorrect placement held just fine until enough pressure was applied. Then the pin was pulled through. Simple enough, but it could have been disastrous.

I re-rigged and was underway within an hour, but had to travel several miles up the ICW to find a place to safely cross the reef, and be on my way to Bimini.

Captain Jack's Complete Navigation, By Jack I. Davis

Captain Jack's Complete Navigation, By Jack I. Davis

Captain Jack's Complete Navigation, By Jack I. Davis

ISLA MUJERES, MEXICO

In late May, with my first mate and a crewman, we had sailed, nonstop, 1600 miles across the Caribbean Sea from Antigua, West Indies, bound for Houston, Texas. When the crewman developed medical problems, we were forced to stop in Isla Mujeres, Mexico to put him on a plane to Houston.

My first mate and I decided to call friends in Houston and ask them to join us for the trip home. They were delighted that we called them.

We decided to play tourist after they arrived, and arranged for our friendly cab driver, Jose "El Negro" Lopez to drive the four of us to the Mayan ruins at Chichén Itzá.

Jose picked us up early the next day. We had a delightful drive to the ruins and spent several hours there.

Jose knew some fabulous restaurants that a tourist would never find. As I mentioned before, my first mate and I are professional eaters, with Mexican food high on our preference list.

The marina was filled with sailboats, mostly from the US or Canada in transit to or from Mexico and Central America. As soon as we arrived we met several of these yachtsmen.

Soon everyone in the marina knew we were a professional delivery crew. We were asked many questions about the weather and whether and if we felt a hurricane was possible.

I assured everyone that June was too early for a hurricane, and I wouldn't give that eventuality a second thought. I was leaving for Houston and had no worries about the weather. We were the only boat headed for Houston -- most of the others were going to Florida and points north.

One Canadian couple, en route from California through the Panama Canal, asked about the Key West area. I recommended a stop at Fort Jefferson in the Tortugas, which is well worth seeing.

His wife was from Jamaica, a place I had sailed by but had never stopped and I was fascinated hearing her stories of that country. I decided it was a place I must visit.

We spent about a half day in Cancun to re-provision for the trip home. Cancun is a "free port," with huge supermarkets that stock more items than stores in the US. They also have items not available in the States, such as canned butter from Holland and fantastic chocolate milk from Denmark.

We left early the next day, as did the Canadian couple. We had a beautiful sail up the Yucatan coast, keeping the Canadian's sail in sight off our starboard beam. The sail slowly got smaller as they drifted east of north.

I didn't see their sail after we made the turn for home at the Yucatan. Looking back toward Cancun, I saw a huge cloud forming. This cloud was entirely too big for this time of year, so I started keeping careful tabs on it. My apprehension growing as fast as the clouds.

My concern grew as the huge system (not a cloud anymore) continued to expand. By mid-afternoon we were looking at an awesome formation, but movement seemed to be slightly to the northeast. Our course was northwest, so it wasn't getting any closer to us.

The first night at sea the winds reached twenty to twenty-five knots and I had to reef. I thought these winds could be related to the system behind us. The movement of that system, possibly our way, worried me.

Morning relieved my anxiety as the winds eased to a more typical fifteen knots and the storm behind us got further away. The weather was favorable for the balance of the trip.

As soon as we got home I heard south Florida had been hit by a hurricane, one of the earliest in the season during recorded history. The people in the marina who took my weather advice will never again take the advice of a professional delivery captain.

The storm I saw was overtaking the Canadians long before they got to Key West. With the aid of charts they pulled into the Fort Jefferson anchorage and were secured before the brunt of the storm hit. They were able to ride it out with no significant damage.

THE MAKING OF A FISHERMAN

Boat deliveries come in all shapes and sizes and from various directions, and this next one, for me, was one of the strangest.

A sailboat owner in the marina where we were berthed asked three other sailboat owners to crew for him on his move to Key West, Florida. Since none of them had been to sea, except as crew, and even that on a limited basis, they decided to call me for assistance.

I viewed their situation, not as a delivery, but more like an advanced sailing lesson. I offered to go at my regular rate, but I would have no watch duties. By doing so I would be free to spend time with each of them, concentrate on teaching and do a little offshore fishing.

Randy the owner agreed, but said, "I don't fish, I don't clean fish, and I don't eat fish!"

The crew consisted of boat owners, Mike, George and Maya. Randy was an electronic junkie possessing a hand-held GPS, big screen GPS, computers with built-in navigation programs, autopilot, single-side band radio, satellite telephone and more.

The four had spent several days getting the boat ready. A thirty-five gallon bladder was installed on the fore deck for reserve diesel fuel. I made only a casual inspection of the boat, checking that everyone had a harness, there were essential engine spares, extra engine oil and plenty of groceries. I asked Randy if he had one or two five-gallon fuel jerry cans. He said with the bladder it wouldn't be necessary. An alarm went off in my head but I didn't act on it -- a big mistake.

Randy said the water tanks were topped off and there was plenty of bottled drinking water. I should have asked, "Is the water in the tanks potable?" That made two errors.

We left at mid-afternoon and motored down the Houston ship channel because the moderate wind was directly in our face. As it got dark and we neared the Galveston jetties, the winds increased rapidly.

By the time we were between the jetties the wind reached thirty knots, and was still right in our face.

An unusual thing can happen when the winds are fairly high, blowing up the channel toward the bay, with a strong outgoing tide, or current. The wind pushes already large waves into mounds, much higher than they would be without the current. In addition to being higher, they are closer together. This is what we ran into that night.

About two-thirds of the way to the end of the jetties, the boat was going down extremely steep seas, almost burying the bow, then virtually straight up to the next top, to suddenly fall into the next trough.

I experienced this before leaving Mobil Bay and again at Pensacola. I was not surprised, but the rest of the crew was horrified at the violent motion.

Randy had gone below to check our position on the computer. The hatch was closed because we had taken green water over the dodger.

I made the decision to reverse course. When I opened the hatch to let Randy know I saw the cabin was in disarray, with gear being thrown everywhere and

Randy was sick. He agreed completely with the course change.

There is a decent anchorage next to the yacht club in Galveston. We anchored there and spent several hours cleaning and re-stowing.

We discovered the bilges full of water and the pumps clogged and not working. It took another hour to clean the pumps and get the water out. Before dozing off, I thought how fortunate we were to have resolved the pump problem in a nice quiet anchorage.

We awoke the next morning to a beautiful, windless day. We didn't know it then, but we had seen the last of the wind all the way to Key West.

The crew decided on watches of three on and nine off, a very relaxed, easy-going schedule. George was to sit through Maya's watch most of the time. As agreed, I spent time with everyone.

Mike reeled in a nice dorado (also known as a dolphin fish) the second day out. Randy was fascinated with the landing and cleaning. I took the filets to the galley to prepare Mahi-Mahi with instant rice.

I sautéed the fish in butter with a little lemon pepper. Dorado is one of the best eating fish in the ocean. The white meat becomes even whiter as it is cooked.

When I handed the plates up to the cockpit I included one for Randy. He slowly took one small nibble, a slightly larger one and then dug in with real gusto. He said, "I had no idea fish could taste this good."

George landed the next fish and Randy was more observant than he had been before. I went through the cooking procedure with him, and he saw cooking fresh fish is easy.

The next day when a fish hit the line, Randy said he wanted to land it, which he did with no problems. When I laid the fish out to filet, Randy asked if he could try it. I agreed, of course. He had come a long way from the guy who wouldn't catch, clean, or eat fish, and in only three days.

While brushing my teeth, using water out of the tap, I realized it didn't taste right. I commented on this to Randy, and was told he never used tank water for anything other than washing or boiling and never cleaned the tanks or added chlorine.

I awoke the next morning with vomiting and severe stomach cramps. Between my carry-on medical kit and Randy's, I was able to get control but it took a very agonizing thirty hours. I was still able to occasionally go out on deck during this terrible scourge and found the crew doing very well without me. We siphoned the diesel from the bladder into the main tank on the third day. It completely filled the main. I calculated we had used more fuel than anticipated. Making Key West without wind was going to be problematic.

I had convinced everyone that they had to see Fort Jefferson in the Dry Tortugas. Since it was not out of our way, the stop would not affect our fuel problem. About noon the fifth day, we entered the anchorage at the fort. The crew was exuberant. The beautiful old fort, clear water, and scores of fish swimming by, created a dreamlike scene.

We spent two days relaxing, swimming and touring the fort. I didn't recommend the stop thinking everyone may not appreciate it as I do. The enthusiasm of the crew was very gratifying. At sundown the second day, we left for Key West, planning to arrive at sun up.

The crew practiced using the hand-held GPS during overnight watches and were surprised at the difficulty they had understanding the procedures. However, they learned a lot from the experience.

At daybreak we had the marina at Key West in sight, when I detected a RPM change. Since we were all in the cockpit, everyone had noticed the change. Mike went forward to stand by the anchor, only a minute before the engine died.

Mike got the anchor over in a hurry. As the anchor rode ran out we saw we were in a four- or five-knot current. There we were, at anchor, at the edge of the channel, with a Chevron fuel sign in sight. If we didn't have the current against us, we probably could have made it. There was nothing to do but launch the dinghy to go for fuel.

I went with Mike because I was the only one who had been to Key West. At the fuel dock they had no fuel containers for sale and ours were in Texas. It was only 7 AM so we had to wait for a local marine hardware store to open at nine. If I had minded my alarm bell at home we would have had one.

I bought the tanks and was back at the fuel dock a few minutes after nine. Mike who had been waiting with the dinghy, said the crew of our boat had called on the VHF radio. They couldn't understand why it was taking us so long. I told Mike to forget it, they weren't going anywhere without us.

After refueling, bleeding the fuel lines and getting the engine started, I wondered how so many people can spend so much time on diesel sailboats and not learn this simple procedure. Maybe it's because they have never run out of fuel, like I do so often.

Key West was supposed to be a temporary stop for Randy, but I could tell he loved it there.

I recently heard that he did not move on, but has adopted Key West as his permanent port. For a man who so loves to catch, clean, and eat fish, it is a great place to be.

Captain Jack's Complete Navigation, By Jack I. Davis

CENTERBOARD NIGHTMARE

I prefer not to have owners aboard during a delivery, but since I teach sailing, and enjoy teaching, I make an exception when the owner goes along for the learning experience.

I make a point that the owner is crew and that the arrangement is not a democratic one. The majority does not rule, nor do I want to debate my decisions.

In actual practice these deliveries have been satisfactory and indeed, the owners have been very complimentary about the experience, with only one or two exceptions.

This next story is one of the good trips, although it was challenging for everyone aboard.

I was met at the Corpus Christi, Texas airport by the proud new owners of a six-year-old, forty-four foot Pearson, center cockpit, centerboard ketch. This couple had several years sailing experience on lakes and they would have had no problem handling their new purchase, but they had never been to sea and weren't comfortable with navigation.

They could have gone through the ICW to their berth on Lake Ponchetrain without help, but they decided it would be worth my delivery fee to get a few days blue water experience. So they had driven to Corpus Christi, spent a few days getting the boat ready and called me.

I found while talking with them that a marine surveyor had just completed his survey of the boat and had found no significant problems other than the usual disclaimers to protect his reputation. I read through the survey then spent about an hour doing my walk-through.

The boat seemed to have been well maintained and I didn't see any obvious signs of abuse. The main things I look for, such as safety jackline, harnesses with whistles and strobe light, plenty of flashlights and other safety equipment, and lots of groceries were all in place.

The water tanks held more than enough water for a four-day trip and the fuel, I thought, was adequate but I made a serious miscalculation. The survey showed a Yanmar diesel engine, a type I have run for thousands of miles. When I looked in the engine room I saw what I thought was the same engine I was familiar with which burns no more than one-half gallon of diesel per hour. The fuel we had on board would have been enough to motor almost all the way to Louisiana if I had been correct.

I didn't know that Yanmar made a sailboat engine almost twice that size, that burned over one gallon per hour and that would cut our motoring range in half.

I gave my little speech about what I expected of crew, set up a watch schedule and said, "Let's get out of here!"

We left the new marina at Port Aransas about noon. From there to the Gulf of Mexico is only a few miles so we had the sails up and were moving briskly along within an hour.

The crew went through the usual excited enthusiasm when the porpoises met us just past the jetties. These characters are always fun to watch as they begin jumping and playing with the bow wave of the boat. The crew grabbed their cameras and shot up several rolls of film, which may or may not show one or two of the elusive animals, but will add to the enjoyment of reliving this experience, never the less.

I love the open waters of the Gulf of Mexico; the indescribable blue the water turns as the bottom falls away, the many different types of birds who put on their show, the porpoise and jumping fish, and the extraordinary freshness the sea air brings to the mixture. It is an added pleasure for me to witness the glee of others who have never seen it before.

They were spellbound by the splendor of the sea that afternoon, then nighttime brought on a whole new dimension of charm as the stars sparkled out, first by the dozens, then by the millions and trillions. Most folks, who live on land, especially in cities, have never seen the sky as it is at sea. Words are inadequate to describe the magnificence.

As it turned out we had a very compatible group. The conversations were vibrant; they appeared interested in my sea stories and they loved to cook good food. As a professional eater I appreciate that talent immensely.

We sailed most of that first night, but before morning the winds began to die down. I had set five knots as the minimum acceptable speed, and when our speed dropped below that I fired up the Yanmar to motor sail, and why not? We have plenty of fuel, I thought.

The second day was pretty much like the first but with more motoring than I like to do. By the third day we had dropped all pretense of sailing, furling the jib and leaving the main up, sheeted in tight, only to dampen the roll.

Almost everything unusual or frightening happens between midnight and 0200, and that third night was no exception. At about 0100 I was at the helm, motoring along at about six knots. The crew was down below snoring away when suddenly something banged into the boat. It sounded and felt like a twenty-foot ChrisCraft doing about fifteen knots had rammed us. Before I could react it banged into us again and again. I pulled the throttle back as fast as I could and as the boat slowed the banging tapered off and finally quit altogether.

My crew raced out on deck saying, "What in the hell is going on?"

My first reaction when something like this happens is to turn on the spreader lights. With the lights on we could tell for sure that there was no ChrisCraft imbedded in our hull, nor were there any obstructions in sight. We were in nine thousand feet of water which pretty well eliminated the oil-field type obstructions.

I have always worried about coming up on a shrimp trawler and getting into his nets but there wasn't a light in sight other than our running lights, and I had not seen another boat all night. I went over and pulled on the line that retracts the centerboard and to my surprise it was as tight as a fiddle string. It should have been slack. I realized then what had happened.

The stainless steel pin that the two-thousand-pound centerboard swiveled on had failed. The centerboard fell off and would have gone rapidly to the bottom except for the small retrieval line, which was never meant to carry all that weight.

All of us sat in the cockpit and mulled this over for a while. Finally I told them that we didn't have a prayer of bringing the centerboard onto the deck. The only way possible would be for a diver to go under the boat and attach a halyard to it, then winch it up. We didn't have scuba gear and there was no way any of us could free dive to do the job. Whether with scuba or free diving, one o'clock in the morning is not a good time to be in the water in the middle of the Gulf.

I knew we couldn't leave it there because when the boat moved, the tethered centerboard would flutter like a leaf, banging into the hull and possibly even knocking a hole in it. I opened my rigger's knife and handed it to the owner. "I'll give you the honor of freeing us from the millstone suspended at the end of the line." Without further fanfare he cut the line.

I didn't have any idea how well the boat would sail without the centerboard, but with very little wind it didn't matter. Before dawn the wind came up enough to sail, so I shut the engine down and found that indeed, she sailed very nicely.

By noon the fourth day the wind had again dropped and we were motor sailing while entering the Morgan City oil field. We were still almost one hundred miles from Grand Isle, Louisiana, but everything was looking rosy.

At about 1400 I detected a slight change in engine speed, which brought the hackles up on the back of my neck. No one else seemed to notice it. Even though I wasn't at the helm I could see the throttle, and no one had touched it.

I have been around these little diesel engines so long that I can sense an RPM change even in my sleep. I walked over to be close to the throttle and within just a few minutes she quit. I pulled the throttle back and hit the kill switch but I was too late, the engine had died from fuel starvation.

I was hoping that we had a stopped-up fuel filter or a plugged up line -- something I could fix -- but I determined right away that the engine had died because we had no fuel.

I had the crew hoist the sails while I got the engine book out. Sure enough, we didn't have the engine I thought we had, but that was now water under the bridge. Or better yet, diesel out the stern.

The wind started picking up and we were making some headway so there wasn't any great immediate concern. I thought that as we got further into the Morgan City oil field we might talk someone out of a little diesel fuel.

By dawn we had good winds and were up over my five knot minimum speed, which was fortunate because, without engine power, we were at the mercy of those winds. We might be able to sail to Grand Isle, but trying to sail through Barataria Pass, not to mention getting into the marina, would be a problem. Also we had used our running lights for one night without replenishing the batteries so we probably couldn't maintain lights another night without recharging.

I started looking for an oil field crew boat or utility boat to beg some fuel.

There was one close to our course at about noon, so I called him on the VHF marine radio. The captain of the eighty-foot utility boat replied. I told him that I had made a serious miscalculation, that we were out of fuel, and could he let us have some?

I have always found these people to be exceptionally helpful through the years, but this time the captain was cool. He said, "I don't have any way to pump fuel to you."

I said, "That's okay, we are sailing good and I think we can make it." Another voice came on the radio, "What type vessel are you?" I replied, "We are a forty-four foot sailboat." That voice asked again, "How much fuel to you need?"

My main concern was for a few hours battery charging time and then about one hour motoring in through the pass, so I answered "Five gallons should do it."

The utility boat captain came back, "Five gallons? Oh hell, I thought you needed a thousand. I'll bring you over five gallons right now."

I had the owner's wife steer a straight course and the utility boat came along side. One of the hands on the utility boat reached out and handed us a five-gallon container of diesel. I tried to pass a ten-dollar bill over to the hand but he laughed and said, "Forget it."

"Do you want your container back?" I asked, and again he laughed and said they had dozens of them.

We put the diesel in and went to the engine room to bleed the engine, which turned out to be a good learning experience for the owner who had never bled a diesel engine.

We recorded the name and company information on the utility boat, and later wrote a letter thanking the company, which we thought might be beneficial to the captain, a sort of pay back for his help.

The engine started with no problems, but we only used it an hour to charge batteries. We sailed through the night and made it to the port about dawn. We then motored in with no other problems except to run aground inside the marina, but it was easy to get off.

Relatives of the owner were on the dock waiting for us and I was on the way to the airport within an hour, another successful delivery out of the way.

Captain Jack's Complete Navigation, By *Jack I. Davis*

CLEAN FUEL

A potential world cruiser's dream of buying his dream boat, going through it from stem to stern, adding dozens of pieces of equipment, and fueling up and casting off went astray right after fueling up.

This was a retiree who bought a new forty-four foot Stamus ketch and spent about a year getting it exactly the way he wanted it to sail off into the soft tropical twilight. Then he died.

The boat sat at the dock for a couple of years, while wills and probate did their thing. Then the boat was for sale for a few months. When a buyer made a deal on the boat he contacted me to deliver it to his home at Ft. Pierce, Florida.

This appeared to be a boat as ready to go as you could ask for. The engine only had twenty-five hours on it and there were spare filters, belts, gaskets, impellers, and on and on. There were a couple of cases of engine oil, extra transmission fluid, extra hydraulic fluid, and the diesel tanks were topped off.

I had to flush and refill the water tanks, put groceries and charts aboard and I was about ready to go. I didn't think about inspecting the fuel tanks, but I should have, although I don't think there was a fuel tank inspection port.

Captain Jack's Complete Navigation, By Jack I. Davis

I had a couple of crew volunteers standing by, which was all the crew I needed, but at the last minute a local sailing instructor asked to go, which really surprised me. He had been teaching for several years on Galveston Bay, but admitted to having almost no blue water experience, so I invited him along.

There was no electronic navigation equipment aboard. I suppose the original owner hadn't gotten around to buying those items so I decided to go with my sextant.

It was mid November, which can be a potentially rough weather crossing in the Gulf of Mexico, but that is the lot of a delivery captain who hardly ever has an option on when to go. I alerted the crew to bring weathers and warm clothing.

I rigged jacklines and fitted the crew with harnesses, showed them how to activate the attached strobe light, and had them try out their whistles. And then we were off.

We had a day and half of typical southeast winds. Then we were overtaken by a cold front with winds of twenty to thirty knots out of the northwest that stayed with us for several days.

The wind was right on our stern and as the wind continued to blow, the seas built to about fifteen feet. A following sea is the most difficult circumstance in which to steer under the best of conditions, but it was far more difficult on this vessel because of hydraulic steering.

The wheel at the helm turned seven revolutions from chock to chock. In the following seas the helmsman had to turn the wheel very rapidly to keep the boat from broaching. Instead of being a mundane and boring job, your turn at the wheel was a lot of work.

We started out on three-hour watches, then cut that down to two, and after a while, even that got to be too much. The temperature was in the mid-forties. Not unpleasant, but with a misty rain we had to wear rain gear, so after about one hour of fighting the helm we would be wringing wet, not from the rain but from perspiration.

About twelve hours after the front hit us, we were really bouncing around. The sailing instructor, Joe, fell from one side of the main salon to the other, apparently breaking some ribs.

He was wearing a white T-shirt, so I encapsulated him in duct tape from his neck to his waist over the T-shirt, and secured him in his bunk, where he stayed until we docked in Key West.

We all pitched in; brought him hot soup, water, coffee and whatever else he needed. This made it hard for us since we were already doing one hour on and three off, but with one man out of commission we were down to one on and two off.

After forty-eight hours of that duty I hove-to for six hours and let everybody get some rest while I kept watch. After we started sailing again, with a much better attitude, the winds started dropping and shifting more to the northeast, which made sailing a pleasure again. We went back to three on and six off.

I had been running the generator one hour, three times each day, to keep the batteries charged. Suddenly, during one of these charging sessions the diesel engine died. Our fuel tanks were still almost full so I went into the engine room to search out the problem.

I found that the primary fuel filter was full of crud, and upon examining it I discovered it was the bacterial slime that occurs in diesel fuel when it sits too long, especially if there's a little moisture in the tanks. In the Houston area the humidity is so high you can depend on the moisture being there.

Everyone adds a biocide chemical to the diesel fuel to prevent the slime from building up -- everyone except the original owner who probably didn't know. I cleaned out the filter and put a new unit in but I still couldn't get a flow of diesel. My first attempt at sucking fuel through the line failed, but on the second attempt I got a flow of fuel and a lot of black slime.

The boat had sat for so long with no biocide in it that there was a profusion of this build up clinging to the sides of the tank. When you examined the fuel and filters everything looked beautiful, but when we got in the following seas, the fuel sloshing around broke this build up loose and it started flowing with the fuel.

I bled the engine and got it started, but it only ran for an hour, then shut down again. My fate was to clean filters, suck diesel fuel through the lines, bleed and restart for each hour of running time all the way to Key West. The good news was that with the horrible diesel taste in my mouth I wasn't hungry so I lost a few pounds.

Of course, the same was true with the main engine when we started it to motor sail. With my other duties of taking sextant sights, tending our injured crew, and standing watch, I was a busy little beaver.

When our DR position showed we were west of the Dry Tortugas I took a sextant sight that showed we were about fifty miles further south than I thought, almost in Cuban waters. I had anticipated the usual two-knot current against us, but with the north wind blowing, that two-knot north set current became a two-knot south set.

I turned and headed for Key West, the closest port, to see if we could resolve our fuel problems. After dark that evening the loom of the city lights of Havana off our starboard beam confirmed our position, and by midnight we could see the loom from Key West.

We pulled into Ocean Side Marina about noon. As I was tying up, our injured crewman, Joe, jumped from the boat to the dock to help out. He had removed his duct tape and evidently had no more pain, which should go down in history as the world's fastest recovery from broken ribs.

I rented a car to run around and buy replacement filters and a few other items, and to find someone to polish our fuel. The rental company let me have a red Dodge convertible at the small car price. With the entire crew, we buzzed around Key West with the top down, like teenagers.

By sundown I had accomplished all my chores and told the crew we should get a good night's rest and leave for Ft. Pierce the next morning. By then I was ready for bed.

Joe asked if it would be all right for him to run around in the car that night. (He was all rested up after several days in his bunk and wanted to see the bikini clad teeny boppers strolling downtown.)

I was too tired to care and let him have the car keys. I don't know what time he came in, nor did I want to know, but we left the next morning for a pleasant sail up the Florida coast that turned out to be absolutely uneventful.

For several days I had a bad taste in my mouth. And the diesel bothered me, too!

Captain Jack's Complete Navigation, By Jack I. Davis

Captain Jack's Complete Navigation, By Jack I. Davis

'COME BACK' LITTLE TEXACO

We had been on the way from Georgetown in the Exumas Island Chain, Bahamas to San Juan, Puerto Rico but stopped at Conception Island for a little diving.

When you say diving you usually mean scuba diving, but scuba diving when you are alone is not safe or practical. When I wanted to look for lobster or grouper, there was rarely any other scuba divers around, so I snorkeled a lot, as did most of the other sailors I knew.

There were several other sailboats in the anchorage at Conception Island. As soon as I announced on the VHF radio the possibility of a lobster and grouper hunting trip there were two other eager divers on the way to my boat. One of these sailors came in a small wooden outboard-equipped dinghy, in which the other two of us gratefully accepted a ride.

Conception Island is out in the Atlantic Ocean with extremely deep water around it. In my other Bahamian diving experiences on the banks, the water was ten to fifteen feet deep for miles in all directions. Riding down the beach in crystal clear water I could see the white sand bottom toward the beach and dark blue water starting right under us.

We finally started seeing a few reefs. Then we had reefs on both sides. We dropped anchor, and went overboard.

I was startled to find how deep the water was. I was accustomed to free diving with a Hawaiian sling and spear in the ten to fifteen foot range. In this area of Conception Island the tops of the reefs were that deep, going on down another fifteen feet to the sand bottom. A trip down there, for me, was a tough challenge.

The beauty of the reefs and sea life was dazzling. There were two or three varieties of sea turtles soaring along in flocks, numerous rays flying by, including a very large spotted ray who glided in very close, and thousands of colorful reef fish, but the caves that should have been inhabited by grouper and lobster were empty.

Each dive took a lot out of me, more than I wanted to admit but I enjoyed every moment of it. After four hours of diving beyond my normal capacity and not finding anything, I was approaching exhaustion when I went down to look in one last cave. There I saw the grandfather of all lobsters.

I was so startled I didn't try to shoot it but just sped to the surface. I hollered at my companions, telling them what I had just seen, got a deep breath and went back down.

It's hard to explain just how large a beast like that looks underwater through a face mask. I would have bet he was bigger than me, but of course he wasn't. I shot him with my spear and had a hard time pulling him out of the cave.

By the time I got him out of the cave I was out of air and still twenty feet down. The spear's lanyard was secured to my wrist so I couldn't get it off, nor could I remove the spear from the lobster, so I paddled as hard and fast as I could and made it to the surface with nothing to spare.

The next problem was getting the lobster into the dinghy. I was as limp as a dish rag and had absolutely nothing left, so I asked one of the guys if he would get in the dinghy and help me load it.

The two other divers wanted to go back and look in the cave to see if there might be more lobster, so they did and found two more, about half as big, but still very large. I was so tired I just lay on the surface with my snorkel up, watching them, and wondering how I was going to get in the dinghy. I thought it would be embarrassing to have to ask the younger guys to help the old man into the very tender dinghy.

The guys loaded the last two lobsters in the dinghy, then went back for one more look into the cave. They didn't find any more so they floated toward the surface. I suddenly saw startled looks on their faces and turned to see what had spooked them.

Swimming toward us was a huge Tiger shark. The water around us was full of lobster blood. This guy was coming in with a different posture than I had ever seen on a shark.

The sharks on the Bahama banks were well-fed, non-aggressive individuals who never gave a diver a second look. This gray monster was coming up out of the very deep water where he had not been well fed. My immediate impression was, "this guy has an attitude."

He came in close and started circling us as we turned to follow his movements. At the same time, we were moving toward the dinghy as fast as we could, but it seemed very far away.

On his last circle he made a fast turn and came straight at us, going under our feet at the last moment. He didn't go far and made another fast turn back toward us. At that same instant I reached up and felt the dinghy. I jumped in without assistance from anyone and the other two guys almost beat me.

We lay there for some time trying to calm down as the shark continued to circle.

When we got back to our boats it was picture-taking time. After several years I got some of the pictures out and my lobster wasn't nearly as big as I remembered him. Maybe the film shrank?

After everyone was fed I made the decision to raise anchor and head for San Salvador. Two of the other boats did likewise. We estimated arriving about midnight, but about two hours before midnight the wind shifted to the north and started a steady increase in speed.

By the time we got to San Salvador we were doing hull speed under reefed sails on a direct course for San Juan, so after a brief discussion on the radio we decided not to stop. The winds continued to increase which kept me on deck reefing, and finally changing to storm sails.

As it turned out I didn't sleep at all that first night and continued to fight the helm until about mid-afternoon, when I finally couldn't take it any more and went below for some rest.

Before I even closed my eyes the helmsman screamed for me to come back on deck. I ran up and asked what the problem was and was told that the winds had gotten much higher, we were going too fast, and the boat was trying to surf.

I had read about other sailors' experience with exhaustion, but didn't think it would ever happen to me. Now I was faced with a fairly simple problem and could not think what to do.

I sat down in the cockpit and thought, "What should I do?" I had a lot of sailing experience, won lots of races, and been in lots of heavy weather, but I was drawing a blank.

Finally I concluded that if I dropped the storm tri-sail, leaving us with just the storm jib, we would probably slow down. And of course we did. After thinking this over for a while I began to grasp the problem and decided to hove-to.

We were pretty far out in the Atlantic by then, outside any shipping lanes with no islands anywhere close, so I dropped our one remaining sail, lashed the helm hard over, and put the hatch boards up.

We slept soundly for about six hours. When I awoke I was laughing at how stupid I had become because of the exhaustion.

The next day the storm continued with steady winds above fifty knots. The waves were gigantic, but nice and orderly and the sailing wasn't that bad. At about mid-afternoon we were pooped for the first time in my sailing career.

I was sitting in the cockpit when at the peak of a mountainous wave the top broke over the boat putting me chest deep in water in the blink of an eye. Getting wet didn't bother me but as I looked down, I saw that my Tiller Master autopilot was under water. When you are short handed, in the middle of a big ocean the most disturbing thing that can happen is losing your autopilot.

The excess water drained out in what seemed like twenty minutes, but in reality was about one minute. I disconnected the autopilot and took it apart. We got out cotton swabs and rubbing alcohol and cleaned and dried with the intensity you would give to saving an injured relative.

I put it back together, hooked it up, crossed my fingers and with a prayer, turned it on. It worked, not exactly right, but it worked, and continued to work, after a fashion, the rest of the way to San Juan.

I called both of the other boats on the radio and got an immediate reply, which surprised me because I thought they would have been far ahead of me and out of range. They were surprised we had stopped and rested, as they both had carried on.

By the fifth day out I was becoming a little concerned about the overcast condition preventing any sextant sights. About mid-afternoon the sun almost made it out, but not quite. Anyway, I tried a sight of the halo of the sun, worked it out and found our DR position was just about right. But I had no idea if that type of sight was dependable.

Within thirty minutes of that sight I spotted a Texaco tanker on the horizon. I asked my crewman to give the tanker a call on the radio and see if he would give us a position report.

I sat at the helm and watched while the crewman down below was talking on the radio.

Suddenly the Texaco tanker made a turn toward us. I couldn't imagine what was going on. I asked the crewman what was said on the radio. The reply was, "I said, 'Texaco tanker, Texaco tanker, this is the sailing vessel Yonder, come back.'"

As it turned out the captain of the tanker was Norwegian and didn't know anything about CB talk. To him "come back" meant, come back!

I got on the radio and apologized, trying to explain that we just wanted a position report, and that we were in no danger of any kind. He seemed to take it pretty well and gave us a position report that confirmed my earlier sight. Then he went on his way and I went on my way chagrined, vowing to never allow CB talk on any VHF marine radio again.

We made San Juan the next morning, almost two days ahead of the other boats.

My first priority after clearing customs was to package the autopilot and ship it to the Tiller Master factory in California. They repaired it and shipped it back in about a month, along with a letter that said, "This instrument is not designed to be used under water of any kind, especially salt water. Do not allow this to happen again."

I promised.

Captain Jack's Complete Navigation, By Jack I. Davis

My thanks to this wonderful class for all their patience and diligent efforts. They were a great inspiration in the writing of this book.

Back Row: Captain Jack I Davis, Al Zucha, Richard Johnson, Gene Salyer.

Middle Row: Dave Quick, Joe McQuade, Photo or Rae McQuade.

Front Row: Pam Russell, Steve Billotte, Ann Taylor.

Captain Jack's Complete Navigation, By Jack I. Davis

Books published by Bristol Fashion Publications
www.wescottcovepublishing.com

Boat Repair Made Easy — Haul Out
Written By John P. Kaufman

Boat Repair Made Easy — Finishes
Written By John P. Kaufman

Boat Repair Made Easy — Systems
Written By John P. Kaufman

Boat Repair Made Easy — Engines
Written By John P. Kaufman

Standard Ship's Log
Designed By John P. Kaufman

Large Ship's Log
Designed By John P. Kaufman

Custom Ship's Log
Designed By John P. Kaufman

Designing Power & Sail
Written By Arthur Edmunds

Fiberglass Boat Survey
Written By Arthur Edmunds

Building A Fiberglass Boat
Written By Arthur Edmunds

Buying A Great Boat
Written By Arthur Edmunds

Outfitting & Organizing Your Boat For A Day, A Week or A Lifetime
Written By Michael L. Frankel

Boater's Book of Nautical Terms
Written By David S. Yetman

Modern Boatworks
Written By David S. Yetman

Practical Seamanship
Written By David S. Yetman

Captain Jack's Basic Navigation
Written By Jack I. Davis

Captain Jack's Celestial Navigation
Written By Jack I. Davis

Captain Jack's Complete Navigation
Written By Jack I. Davis

Building A Fiberglass Boat
Written By Arthur Edmunds

Daddy & I Go Boating
Written By Ken Kreisler

Captain Jack's Complete Navigation, By Jack I. Davis

My Grandpa Is A Tugboat Captain
Written By Ken Kreisler

Billy The Oysterman
Written By Ken Kreisler

Creating Comfort Afloat
Written By Janet Groene

Living Aboard
Written By Janet Groene

Simple Boat Projects
Written By Donald Boone

Racing The Ice To Cape Horn
Written By Frank Guernsey & Cy Zoerner

Boater's Checklist
Written By Clay Kelley

Florida Through The Islands What Boaters Need To Know
Written By Captain Clay Kelley & Marybeth

Marine Weather Forecasting
Written By J. Frank Brumbaugh

Basic Boat Maintenance
Written By J. Frank Brumbaugh

Complete Guide To Gasoline Marine Engines
Written By John Fleming

Complete Guide To Outboard Engines
Written By John Fleming

Captain Jack's Complete Navigation, By Jack I. Davis

Complete Guide To Diesel Marine Engines
Written By John Fleming

Trouble Shooting Gasoline Marine Engines
Written By John Fleming

Trailer Boats
Written By Alex Zidock

Skipper's Handbook
Written By Robert S. Grossman

Wake Up & Water Ski
Written By Kimberly P. Robinson

White Squall - The Last Voyage Of Albatross
Written By Richard E. Langford

Cruising South
What to Expect Along The ICW
Written By Joan Healy

Electronics Aboard
Written By Stephen Fishman

A Whale At the Port Quarter
A Treasure Chest of Sea Stories
Written By Charles Gnaegy

Five Against The Sea
A True Story of Courage & Survival
Written By Ron Arias

Captain Jack's Complete Navigation, By Jack I. Davis

ABOUT THE AUTHOR

Captain Jack I. Davis and his first mate Mary (Mary is an excellent sailor and registered nurse) have lived aboard their forty-three foot Wauquiez ketch since 1984.

His first career was banking and his second career was computer software for banks but his main love has always been sailboats. During this time he owned several power boats and enjoyed water skiing and fishing but yearned for the blue water which the Texas lakes did not offer.

He had made several ocean crossings before obtaining his first U. S. Coast Guard Captain's License in 1984 at which time he started boat deliveries in earnest. The majority of the deliveries have been from Texas to Florida and the West Indies with one delivery completely circumnavigating the Gulf of MexicoBetween deliveries he has taught countless sailing and navigation classes. His sense of humor and teaching style, as demonstrated in this book, keep his students coming back for more.

He has continually upgraded that first license and now holds a U. S. Coast Guard Master's License, Steam, MotorSail and Sail.

www.ingramcontent.com/pod-product-compliance
Lightning Source LLC
Chambersburg PA
CBHW020646230426
43665CB00008B/336